The Gettysburg Experience:

Contemporary Realities
of the Past as a
Civil War Battlefield

John G. Sabol
C.A.S.P.E.R. Research Center

Also by John Sabol

Ghost Excavator (2007)

Ghost Culture (2007)

Gettysburg Unearthed (2007)

Battlefield Hauntscape (2008)

The Anthracite Coal Region (2008)

The Politics of Presence (2008)

Bodies of Substance, Fragments of Memory (2009)

Phantom Gettysburg (2009)

Digging Deep (2009)

The Re-Haunting(s) of Gettysburg (2010)

The Haunted Theatre (2011)

Ghost Culture Too (2012)

Beyond the Paranormal (2012)

Digging-Up Ghosts (2nd publishing, 2013)

Burnside Bridge (2013)

The Gettysburg Experience:

Contemporary Realities of the Past as a Civil War Battlefield

Ghost Excavator Books, Inc™©

Bedford, Pennsylvania, USA

Dedication

Photo 1: My daughter, Melissa, and I, Gettysburg (1995).

With the 150th anniversary of the battle of Gettysburg soon approaching, it is important to salute those men, women, and boys who sacrificed so much on that landscape: those who fought, suffered, and were traumatized, those who died and were properly buried, and those who remain and/or whose remains remain buried, somewhere lost on the battlefield. Their noble acts of courage, commitment, and endurance will endure long after the anniversary has past!

The continued fascination with Gettysburg continues through TV productions, movies, reenactments, living history demonstrations, public displays, battlefield rehabilitation, heritage tourism, paranormal gatherings, and yes "ghost hunting". While not all of these venues are equally meaningful, or involve the same goals and purpose, all do focus on how the battle (and the history of Gettysburg) becomes a lasting remembrance of the importance of what happened here, and who occupied (still occupies) this Gettysburg landscape.

This book is a memory to what (and "who") may still remain, what's left from that battle, and what came before and after. My intention is meant to be therapeutic and respectful. There is no other way, given what those who walked this landscape once endured. I salute all of them, and hope that all are at peace......or soon will be!

Photo 2: A "Noble" Death on the Field of Battle

At Gettysburg, the past has caught-up with the present…………..

But whose past is it…………..?

Preface

"Some eye that never saw the battle will select, and some pen will write what will be named the history".

- **Frank A. Haskell (1908:181-82)**

As Haskell's statement implies, we must be very cautious, extremely vigilant, and be meticulous in our research as to the kinds of relevant questions we ask, and purposeful fieldwork we do at Gettysburg. This is especially important when analyzing the primary sources. Leone and Potter (1988), both archaeologists, have effectively argued that those who produced the historical record usually were <u>not</u> the same individuals who created it.

The uncertainty of what remains will likely be reflected in the material culture of those who occupied this history. This requires "digging-deep" into the "Gettysburg Experience". The research value of these archival and fieldwork "excavations" lies in the relationship of manifestations of presence as contemporary experience, and that experience as <u>directly</u> relative to the people and times of Gettysburg's historical record. This is the simple, but often difficult to document, link to past presence: features directly experienced on the ground in specific spaces are relative to the real manifestations of past (and continuing) acts of human beings. Yet, this <u>is</u> what the "Gettysburg Experience" must be.

Henry Glassie (1977) has stated that **"the past is too important to leave to historians. The human reality is too important to leave to the novelists" (1977:32).** I would add to this that the haunting reality of Gettysburg is too important to leave to the "ghost hunters"! We must establish a <u>cultural</u> (not "paranormal") history of the "Gettysburg Experience", a **"ghost culture" (Sabol 2008)** of what remains from multiple pasts. This exploration of the "ghost culture" of Gettysburg must become a "ghost culture ethnography" of the continuing expression of past presence within the "Gettysburg Experience".

Visiting a place like Gettysburg, the town as a contemporary "living" community, and the "dead" fields of mostly silence outside the town, offers scores of ghostly evocations. These are not necessarily spontaneous "paranormal" incidents. These ghostly evocations have become (all too frequently) staged events of the Civil War, forming a major everyday (and normal) cultural landscape at Gettysburg.

In the April 2013 issue of Smithsonian Magazine, Gettysburg is ranked first among the 20 **"most intriguing small towns to enjoy arts and smarts"**. The criterion for this choice was based on a small town's **"exceptional concentrations of museums, art galleries, orchestras, theaters, historical sites, and other cultural blessings"**. Why, then, is Gettysburg associated with a large (almost exclusive) Civil War experience, with a focus (based on nine active ghost tour companies) on Civil War haunting experiences?

Walking past the town, and onto a tourist-perceived battlefield, it reveals to the visitor (and investigator alike) hundreds of monuments, memorials, historical plaques on buildings, and sites of memory and lore. All of these settings contain various traces of the past in the present. Interspersed between these historical references are the "paranormal" landmarks, cited in books, during tours, on websites and social media, and in ghost-hunting lore. All of these venues are the "Gettysburg Experience", combining myth, folklore, history, and uncanny experience.

Where the story begins and where reality becomes a manifesting presence, is the central theme of this book. Also contained within these pages is a second major theme: the question of uncertainty. Is it ghostly or historic, belonging to the Civil War era, or does it pre/postdate July, 1863? What (and "who") is really manifesting here? Is it a "mind game", a "trick" of the imagination; or is it a "treat" of re-enactment, a ghostly "wargasm"? Or is it the real thing, an authentic "apparitional experience"?

The Ghost Tours create future hauntings and make manifest contemporary haunted sites. The reports of anomalous experiences can trigger similar experiences in other individuals who subsequently visit a site. Haunt phenomenon are more likely to occur at sites with multiple individuals (McClenon 2001), such as a ghost tour/group investigation.

The identification of a particular site as "haunted" can influence the perceptions by participants, as well as by investigators (Lange and Horan 1997). Contagion/suggestibility effects are enhanced on these tours/investigations through a restricted environment, investigations/tours at night, and the periods of silence between perceived manifestations (Cardena and Spiegel 1991).

The "Gettysburg Experience" is more than a "ghost tour" or a "ghost hunt". The landscape is an active historical museum of continually-evolving exhibits, some remaining more permanent than others (such as the Civil War period). The landscape contains an array of signs, symbols, and manifestations (both spectral and mundane) that can be read and experienced within a cultural context.

This context reveals different human values for different times, each with a variety of meanings, suggestive of particular groupings of motives and goals. To view Gettysburg historically, rather than a static contemporary presence, is to acknowledge the cumulative character of the landscape's various occupations. It is also an understanding of the fluidity of the historical record that becomes intertwined tightly to experience.

What exists today is what survives the death of certain pasts, and the addition of new sets of formed presences. Some call this a "haunting", but speaking from an archaeologically-sensitive perspective, it is a stratigraphy of presence, the ethno-archaeological record of the "Gettysburg Experience". This is a view of the Gettysburg landscape as a process (a living entity), not just a "product" of a particular time (and offering particular goods and services).

As philosopher De Certeau declares:

"There is no place that is not haunted by many different spirits, hidden there in silence, spirits one can 'invoke' or not".

At Gettysburg, most of these "spirits" are <u>not</u> invoked. It is people who create these ghosts and hauntings, not the ghosts who haunt the landscape. Humans create haunted places, as they become contemporary eyewitnesses (and earwitnesses) to the past. At Gettysburg, it is largely the Civil War past. If ghosts were the creators of Gettysburg's haunted places, why is Gettysburg, with a long and varied cultural and ethnic history, mainly haunted by perceived Civil War ghosts?

The memory of the Gettysburg historical record is not merely the acquisition of historical information from a particular space/place, or listening to stories told in the present about some aspect of the past. A memory, as past experience, is a self-reflexive act, not an <u>imposed</u> act. It is contextualized by "digging" down through a site's occupational layers. It is an action of continuous re-experiences that re-make that past (a particular one) present again.

The marketing of Gettysburg today is viewed largely as a one-dimensional exhibit of what <u>particular</u> ghosts of the past should be (continuously) invoked, what past should be remembered, and which presences forgotten. In this way, the Gettysburg landscape, and its parallel "Gettysburg Experience", becomes inhabited (and experienced) by a particular haunting presence. Civil War "ghost soldier" stories fill the empty spaces, providing presences that replace the absent experience of battle.

The Civil War re-presentation of Gettysburg articulates, as well as obscures, other human haunting experiences. Those who visit Gettysburg (in any capacity) must pay added attention to these other "abandoned" spaces and experiences that are not well-placed in the dominant representation of Gettysburg as a Civil War landscape. They must do this, if they hope to seek a well-rounded experience.

To merely imagine Gettysburg through an idealized, selective past (the Civil War) is destructive. It "ruins" the range of different meanings, temporalities, and social spaces that make (and define) Gettysburg as a unique and certainly historically-complex place of experience.

The "Gettysburg Experience" is perceived at many different levels. It has national, international, regional, local, individual, and some highly personal contexts. To understand these contexts, and the appearance of past presence, we must explore and "dig" through the numerous and varied contextual strata and historical narratives.

The existence of the "Gettysburg Experience", as a "ruin" of decaying vestiges and traces of multiple pasts, firmly grounds presence into symbolic meanings of a legitimate past. Gettysburg, as this ruined landscape, helps us to trigger "imagineerings", and inspire reflections on these varied cultural occupations. Lowenthal, in his ground-penetrating book, **The Past is a Foreign Country (1985)**, reminds us of the following:

"Remembering the past is crucial for our sense of identity….to know what we were confirms what we are…." (1985:197).

What we are is not a "ghost". What we are is a presence that haunts. And this presence has haunted the Gettysburg landscape for centuries, and not only since 1863!

This is a book about transformations. It is the Gettysburg battlefield becoming a setting of identities remaining in place. It is also a landscape in which ongoing memories play a pivotal role. Gettysburg today is an "unsettled" notion of place and identity. Thus, those who walk here circulate within the frame of a "becoming", as these identities fluctuate in and out of spaces on the battlefield. The battlefield is a landscape that haunts because it is being unmade and remade through a complex interplay between its past and the events and acts of contemporary moments.

Our relation with this transforming Gettysburg, and our interactions on the battlefield, is a matter of ethics. This ethics addresses how we live and act with each other, and with those past lives of individuals who have lived, fought, and died here. We must remember this when we consider the intimate relation of space, battlefield, affect, emotional attachment, imagination, presence, and identity in Gettysburg.

This is an alternative story (not a "paranormal" one) of what occurred in Gettysburg in 1863. It is not so much an historical account, as it is a creation myth. The "eyes" and "pens" mentioned by Haskell, who fought at Gettysburg, are manifesting today in the narrative accounts (and on social networks) of the "ghost hunters" of contemporary Gettysburg. This is an analysis of that alternative history of the battle, a history that, according to the mythology, manifests today at numerous locations in the town and in the fields surrounding Gettysburg. This alternative history is for now the "popular history" of contemporary Gettysburg. This "popular version" is the basis of "ghostly" myth-building because, it has been said, when **"popular history sings of events and makes them great, it transcends the realm of record and enters that of myth" (McRandle 1944:53-54).**

Gettysburg, as a sense of place and a landscape of battle, has changed through the years. It has evolved from one derived from historical and oral narratives to one of immersed "embodiment". This has become a transition from a "re-enacted experience" to a "reliving" of the past, as embodied in its perceived "haunted" locations. This is a history of a social engagement with a landscape that has transformed from historical description and passive (contemplative) experiences, to one of deep penetration and a personal encounter with the past. This encounter is bound-up with remembrance, memory, and resonance. Its construction is tied into networks of associations, and has largely become a subjective experience.

As humans create, modify, and move through a spatial milieu, the mediation between experience and perception creates and legitimizes the social reality that is associated with a landscape setting. But, at Gettysburg, is this social reality a "haunted" landscape?

At Gettysburg, there are perceived "other" <u>simultaneous</u> landscapes present there today, most notable a "hauntscape" and a "soundscape" of battle. These "scapes" are largely unseen but, in the last two decades, they have been frequently heard from as a form of simultaneous presence equal in appearance, in some cases, to the present.

These other "scapes" have become quite common in contemporary Gettysburg lore, such that a "phantom army" of war, rather than an individual haunting "ghost", has created a particular style of haunting past. This creation is a stylization of battlefield space as contemporary presence, not past history. These presences, rather than viewed as often hidden, are perceived to populate the field of battle as an army to be reckoned with. It has created a "spectral turn" of events at Gettysburg, a move away from a completed history in books to a continuing history that is competing with the official records of the Civil War.

It is the purpose of this book to "excavate" this alternative history in order to "expose" or "recover" these "haunting presences" through the reality of scientific practice, one that is framed within its contextual cultural and social setting. Here, at Gettysburg, myth and history intertwine freely in these fields of drama, and it will take extensive excavations to "unearth" and separate each myth from history, each legend from its archaeological layer, and each folkloric element from its true ethnographic reality. Only then can we identify the meaning and significance of a "haunted" Gettysburg battlefield.

Photo 3: The Gettysburg Battlefield, July 1863.

Photo 4: The Gettysburg Battlefield, 2013.

"And so good-bye to the war…..future years will never know the seething hell and the blank internal background of countless minor scenes…..of the secession war and it is best. They should not. The real war will never get in the books".

- **Walt Whitman**

Is it a real Civil War that remains as a major characteristic of the "Gettysburg Experience", or has a "ghost war" become a part of popular culture today, a form of "zombie walk"? Let us explore together that question in this book……

Introduction 1: Some Theoretical Musings

Is There Space for a "Ghost" in a Place Like Gettysburg?

Gettysburg is an unstable and uncanny place because the spatial practices, regarding its historical character, give multiple expressions (re-enactment, heritage tourism, ghost tourism, living history demonstrations, ghost hunting) that forfeit stability and order. The Gettysburg landscape is a transforming system because these spatial practices operate as <u>different</u> transforming orders, whether that activity be walking, re-enacting, reading, observing, contemplating, participating, or "hunting". Thus, different (and sometimes incompatible) practices in this landscape space are realized, allowing for complex possibilities to be realized in a single place called Gettysburg.

The haunted nature of Gettysburg is modified by these transformations, caused by different contexts of acts. Thus, Gettysburg, as a multi-practiced place, is inherently unpredictable regarding the appearance of past presence as an authentic "apparitional experience". An accurate (and historically-sound) perception of the past, the experience of a haunting, and its authenticity in the context of these practices of transformation, become difficult to determine.

In this sense, as spaces defined as fluid, shifting, and transient, lies the popular appeal of Gettysburg as a haunted location of significant renown. The very <u>constructed</u> (not "paranormal") nature of Gettysburg's transforming elements of role, identity, and social practice has led, in large measure, to the growth of Gettysburg as a mecca for ghost sightings. The Gettysburg haunted landscape has become, not a map of <u>interactive</u> ghost sites, but a map of the various states of mind processed at Gettysburg (re-enactment, historical, recreational, theatrical, and "paranormal"). The question is this "Where" do the real "ghosts" enter into this map?

Table of Contents

Photographs

Introduction 2: Background

The Gettysburg "Spiritscape": No "Escape" from Reality?

Cultural expression as "materialization", and the corresponding experience of it, has materialized in different ways and forms of engagement throughout history, and among different social groups. Basic to these various past material remains, and philosophies that interpret them, is how they make sense today. What becomes the means to "unearth", interact with, and understand the meaning of what is left and "known" (and therefore can be "controlled" as to its interpretation), and how to react to something that is not known? How do we interpret what remains a "mystery"?

One "mystery" that remains a common theme among cultural groups, past and present, is the "spirit world". Archaeologist Christopher Tilly, in a book written decades ago (1999), recognized that landscapes have the potential to go beyond a visual perspective. Landscapes contain more than the architecture and monuments that are built upon them, more than the ruins that remain, and still more of a sense of place they occupy in the archaeological and/or public imagination. Tilly urged a consideration of other **"scapes"** beyond the "landscape".

This possibility of other "scapes" (not "other" dimensions of space/time), opens the door of reality, and the documentation and interpretation of experience in the same space. There are multiple possibilities: "smellscapes", "touchscapes", and "soundscapes", among others. And there are other and varied means in which to conceptualize the meanings of a manifesting presence and "unearthed" remains that are contained in these "scapes". To not take into full consideration these other "scapes" is to <u>escape</u> from reality.

Rupert Sheldrake, in a provocative and controversial book, *The Science Delusion* (2012), warns us that there is no one science, or one exclusive, all-encompassing scientific methodology:

"There are many sciences and many natures. There is no one 'scientific method'; different sciences use different methods" (2012:320).

In a recent article in **LiveScience.com,** skeptic Benjamin Radford states that because the standard of evidence is so low in "ghost hunting", investigators often find "evidence", but not "proof". He further comments that the less the scientific methods are, the more likely this "evidence" becomes.

Let me address these two ideas expounded by Radford. First, "evidence" is for a court of law, <u>not</u> science. Second, he needs to define "scientific methods". His mention of scientific methods is a "blanket" statement, without providing specific disciplinary methodologies of science in which fieldwork can/should be conducted at haunted locations. There are exceptions to his general statement (cf. Nesbitt and Ramsland 2012).

However, too often the concept of "modernity", with its narrow materialist viewpoint of binary opposition is used to express reality, such that we have:

- Us vs. the "other";
- Past vs. present vs. future;
- Alive vs. dead;
- Human vs. "ghost" (or "spirit");

- Paranormal vs. normal; and
- Investigator (as "subject") vs. "anomaly" (as "object").

The question of the verification of "para-normal" reality or "para-normal" event, a process that is the hallmark of any scientific inquiry, becomes the documentation of change from this "other" to what is now considered "normal". Instead, the process should involve an expansion, not transformation to, the reality, not "normality".

At Gettysburg, for several decades now, there have been reports of "ghostly" manifestations of this other "scape", a "hauntscape". The extent and variety of experiences suggest the possibility of a different cultural logic at work here. But is this different cultural logic a historical Civil War "culture of war" consciousness, or is it a contemporary "ghost hunting" culture that is being impressed onto the Gettysburg landscape? Is this a new "hauntscape" emerging (the contemporary), or a manifestation of past social and mental fields (a true "spiritscape")? This book is an examination of that question.

In order to experience a true reality in terms of a "spiritscape", we must immerse ourselves into the "ethnoscape" of the Gettysburg battlefield. This means that we must become knowledgeable of this past ethnographic culture, the "culture of war" of the American Civil War. This includes:

- Its military fields of behavior or Inherent Military Probability (I.M.P.), or how the soldier would have performed in certain situations, and what he would have experienced;
- Its spaces (K.O.C.O.A.) in which this behavior would have been performed; and
- The experience of battle and the battlefield as a "soundscape" and not a landscape.

At Gettysburg, is there an "afterlife consciousness" (a "ghost") of the "culture of war" (a "ghost culture") that manifests I.M.P. behaviors in particular battlefield K.O.C.O.A. spaces (a Gettysburg "spiritscape")? Are the sounds of distant "thunder" one hears on the battlefield just a weather pattern, or do they signal the continuation of a battle long thought completed? This book will help YOU to decide!

The Deep Map: Coming to Our Senses Concerning Haunting Experiences

The use of a "deep map" is an effective strategy in the analysis of the Gettysburg haunting experience. This is because a "deep map" incorporates multiple fields of occupation as a layered experience. It provides various spheres of discourse. In using a "deep map", the politics of vision, though present, is not a privileged (or biased) investigative tool. Deep mapping provides the parameters necessary for a holistic approach in the perception of, and experiences in, a haunted landscape. Some of the elements of a "deep map" include:

- Autobiographical events;
- Routine/mundane activities and cultural habits/practices;
- Traces and vestiges of physical past presence;
- Memories of local places/spaces;
- Ethnic folklore;
- Natural history;
- Ethnographic insights;
- Intuition; and a
- Landscape transforming sensitivity/sensibility.

An example of the use of a "deep map" is the exploration of the "spirit of place" on Monte Altare, Italy (De Nardi 2007). In this analysis, various different (and overlapping) meanings and perceptions of the Monte Altare landscape are presented. The use of these multiple fields capture the complex "faces" of the physical and cultural setting, and evoke meanings **"not as the ghost(s) of places buried and forgotten, but as the living, thriving experience of 'being there'" (De Nardi 2007:12).**

A "deep map" is a cultural, historical, and habitual use of one's experiences and memories of interactions in a particular physical setting. In our normal routine of living, our experiences become narrowly-framed because our perception of the environment is restricted by the range our sensory organs provide of a particular situation. Our actions and activities are also subject to the normal contemporary spatial and temporal boundaries. Without the use of a "deep map", our vision of the multiple presences of the past cannot be sensed, or available for direct experience. A "deep map" also utilizes the concept of **"morphogenetic fields" (Sheldrake 2012).** These "morphogenetic fields" connect similar (resonating) elements across space and time (Sheldrake 1990:117).

What this means is that the use of a "deep map", applied to the concept of "morphogenetic fields", and using the concept of resonance, can provide a multi-sensory approach to the experience of past presences at a location. Past memories may be "interacted" with and, according to Sheldrake, **"these memories need not be stored inside the brain (1990:118).** What this means is that **"both the self and its memories could survive the death of the body" (Ibid: 120).** It may be possible, then, through the use of resonating elements, to **"tune-in to the experience of particular people in the past who are now dead" (Sheldrake 1990:120).**

The multiplicity of occupations of the Gettysburg landscape warrants a typology of engagements with these presences, in which various temporal dimensions are percolating. These fields of past presences should be envisioned as occurring in various spaces at Gettysburg, and forming an integral part of the contemporary "Gettysburg Experience".

Where is "Haunted" Gettysburg?

A. The Horizontal Dimension

Where is the contemporary battlefield? Most people will know that it is located in southeastern Pennsylvania in and around the town of Gettysburg. This may seem like an obvious answer. Since the Civil War, however, the battlefield has been perceptually transformed and translated into multiple, and often conflicting, representations. In these mediations, the "where" is also located "elsewhere" from the town. Mention of the battlefield can be found in books, photographs, video games, on internet websites, and on film and TV. It is also the location "where" many believe Civil War soldiers still continue to engage in battle. "Where" are they (physically) in this continuing conflict?

In this book, I am concerned with the "where" of this Gettysburg "haunted" landscape, as it is perceived to exist and function today, with its "occupying" past presences on the battlefield. Each "presence" represents a field of potential engagement with a haunting uncertainty. And each one defines a particular "where" in this haunted landscape. What haunts the battlefield is <u>not</u> a single and easily measured past presence located in time (the Civil War). There are multiple haunting uncertainties that exist <u>simultaneously,</u> and are located within different layers of this uncertainty, scattered throughout the "hauntscape" that we call "Gettysburg".

Those who attempt to walk with the "spirits" of Gettysburg travel a certain path toward uncertainty. This is no ghostly warning. What is sensed, recorded, measured, and photographed here may not be what one thinks or believes it is. And it may not be located "where" you think they are (or are "perceived"). Understanding is a daunting task. The effort is full of loopholes, obstacles, and changing environments, both cultural and physical. One must be very careful "where" one treads. This is a landscape "where" ghosts exist. Whether these "ghosts" are real or imagined is "where" this book is headed.

The study of Gettysburg's haunting uncertainties must be approached as a non-evasive archaeological "excavation". It involves the use of the **"archaeological imagination" (cf. Shanks 2012).** This "excavation" necessitates particular participatory field practices that "target" a specific strata of this uncertainty. For example, for the uncertainty of continuing Civil War presence, it comprises a particular cultural event (a Civil War battle), activities (the Inherent Military Probability or I.M.P. of a soldier's behavior), and individuals (specific soldiers who fought and died here). A typical "ghost hunt", with its emphasis on the horizontal, cannot differentiate and distinguish between this uncertain Civil War presence and the uncertainties of these other various layers of strata and presence.

Today, the Gettysburg battlefield no longer occupies any one place in history, be it Civil War or "paranormal" history. The battlefield is a heterogeneous and symmetrical ensemble of many uncertainties. It forms part of a complex network of associations and social interactions, both past and present, within these layers of uncertainty. The means to engage this uncertain phenomenon is both varied and complex. Because of this issue of complexity, I suggest that we must move away from a perspective that focuses on merely documenting a continuing Civil War combat and a lingering 1863 ghostly presence.

An excavation into this haunted space does not offer the excavator a linear historical narrative, but rather a topography (a "spectral geography") of particular past remains. A "ghost excavation" seeks to answer the uncertainty of what (and "who") really remains within these multiple fields. A larger question is this: why do only particular fragments of these multiple fields re-appear, while others remain buried and absent from the present? Is what one views at Gettysburg a biased perception, or the reality of a "haunting"? One possible hypothesis to answer this question is offered by Griffin (1997), who says:

"survival with (limited) agency – to explain the basic features of all the (haunting) **phenomena" (1997:266).**

Though manifesting presence appears limited, as suggested by Griffin, much of what may exist as haunting phenomena at Gettysburg is still <u>not</u> being recorded and experienced there. This is because most "ghost hunters" do not view the Gettysburg landscape as an aggregate mix of multiple (and different) past presences. They principally "target" the Civil War era.

Addressing the complexity that may be a certainty at Gettysburg requires an "excavation" that is <u>not</u> directed around histories of distance (the past as "past") and division (absence or presence), but rather toward the unearthing of ontologies that involve strata (layering), context (historical and cultural), association (cultural resonance), and matrix (ethnographies of (past) communication). This is an "archaeological S.C.A.M.".

The "excavation" must also be performative. It must involve the performances of investigators as cultural actors. Though they are here and now, their actions must express empathy <u>and</u> resonance to there and then. The investigative act in the present must resonate with a similar act that occurred in the past. It must be performed, directed at a specific individual, and enacted in an appropriate battlefield space (such as the K.O.C.O.A. (see below)). This creates <u>recognition</u> of identity, and <u>recall</u> of memory, I propose, by any past presence that may remain from the past.

The multi-temporal mixtures of past presences that may remain at Gettysburg constitute various fields in which "ghost excavations" can operate and perform. The "excavation" has a greater possibility, I propose, of "unearthing" an individual presence that may be contained within these symmetrical uncertainties.

The Gettysburg battlefield (which includes the town) is a gathering place that goes temporally beyond linear time, and the physical limits of the contemporary landscape. The "ghosts" of the battlefield are here and elsewhere. They are "liminally"-situated, betwixt and between past and actuality. This is a form of haunting that is still becoming manifest and, to a large degree, have their origin in contemporary activity.

Landscapes, including the Gettysburg landscape, are physical settings where the past (perhaps multiple pasts) accumulate, and its haunted nature is derived from human actors and actions. Landscapes embody these past actions as cultural memories, and are embodied in individual personalities. This haunting character of the landscape can be actualized, in some cases, through material remains that evoke a sense of the past in the mind of a visitor.

We cannot restrict, however, the haunted nature of a landscape to only human actions. A "haunting" is part of our human nature. The natural environment, because of certain physical characteristics, is often "read" by people as a recurring manifestation of an "active" past presence. These are "place memories" that are imprinted upon the environment. All landscapes, therefore, are transformed by human actions and natural processes of growth, decay, and change.

The Gettysburg landscape is no exception. Haunted energy signatures, as materializing residual remains, exist in many spaces on the battlefield. This is a process of de-materialization (absence) and re-materialization (presence). This is because the Gettysburg landscape (or any landscape) can evoke, or hide, its past presence. This is also directly linked to the social environment of mediated remembrance (battlefield memorials), and contemporary memory practices (re-enactments, historical and ghost tourism, "living history" displays/demonstrations, and "ghost hunting").

The possibilities are continuing for the expansion of this "haunting" at Gettysburg. A space, even a well-known historic battlefield such as Gettysburg, can have multiple socially-transforming elements. These transformations insure that "being" and "becoming" are still in a state of flux at Gettysburg.

As an archaeologist, I can look at any given moment in the physical spaces of the Gettysburg battlefield, before and after 1863, with an understanding that all of those past (and present) moments (and the relations that they imprint) are part of an active transforming process as to "where" the battlefield is today. This is important. It means that what (or "who") is present today may not manifest there in the future. This depends upon what occurs between "now" and the future "then".

It is always the contemporary practices that leave the strongest "imprint" upon the "actual" (contemporary) environment. This is a long-standing principle in archaeological excavation: the principle of stratigraphic succession. A haunting is not confined to the present presence (and its unobstructed continuation) of only one particular past, no matter how bloody, emotional, and deadly it was.

An engagement with the Gettysburg past, and its presences, must (by implication) begin from a contemporary perspective, even though multiple pasts occur on the surface of the battlefield. Still, one's "excavation" must work down from the contemporary to the historical because the haunting layers of presence are continually being "built-up".

The contemporary battlefield is a complex stratum of these haunting layers. The "where" a particular haunting originates is the principal goal of a "ghost excavation". This is not a simple horizontal measurement and scan of the ambient environment. It requires a focused "excavation" strategy of each layer of haunting uncertainty. This is a focus on the haunting "S.C.A.M.".

Gettysburg is an accumulative landscape. It contains the vestiges and traces ("sensory remains") of multiple present and past human actions, as well as the natural processes of the locale. The combination of human act and natural action has created an archaeological "ruin" of the battlefields past presences. The Gettysburg battlefield is a checkerboard series of multiple presences and absences. This means that Gettysburg is simply more than a former Civil War battle zone!

The multiple "fields" (both cultural and mental) of Gettysburg contains varying strata of embedded memories. Any investigation there must confront the reality of these layered strata of accumulated memories. This goes beyond simple "ghost hunts". And the fieldwork, as "excavation", is deeper than any individual memory, photograph, or measurement.

The Gettysburg battlefield is a palimpsest. It is a "recorded" document of occupation from multiple pasts that have been written and re-written several times. There, a vast field of diverse memories are located, and is "where" the remains of earlier events, acts, and experiences are not completely erased, but merely suppressed. They can still be unearthed in certain spaces on the battlefield. This does not mean, however, that all of these past occupations and situations still linger on the battlefield.

This understanding of Gettysburg as an accumulative landscape requires an archaeological sensitivity. It necessitates an "unearthing" of its multi-layered strata, layer by layer. This becomes, not a "hunt" for a phantom presence, but an "excavation" of the processes which initiate these past presences to materialize. It is fieldwork based on transformations, the "re-haunting" of Gettysburg throughput its history.

The Gettysburg battlefield, as a contemporary historic entity, goes beyond the simple flow of interest from visitors, the curious, and investigators. It is <u>also</u> a created battlefield. It has become a landscape of monuments, more than 1300 in all. Gettysburg has also been re-created. One current element of this re-creation in recent years has been the National Park Service design strategy of "battlefield rehabilitation". These landscape strategies and design re-adjustments have all affected the haunted character of the battlefield. And these haunting alterations are the norm of a transformative process that will continue at Gettysburg into the future.

Photo 5: Battlefield Rehabilitation at Gettysburg

The differing types of transformations that have occurred in history on the Gettysburg battlefield (historical, hallowed, commemorative, natural, socio-cultural, touristic, monumental, re-created, rehabilitated, haunted, and "hunted" to name a few), although often interacting and overlapping, provide an important theoretical baseline for analyzing the meaningful ways in which both past and present memories (and future designs) are produced and re-produced through human (and natural) acts on the battlefield. They also illustrate how the future haunting character of the battlefield is still in a state of "becoming", not "being".

This haunted character is not a static recording of past (or contemporary) presence, or merely an unchanging and repetitive expression of this presence. It is mobile. This mobility, however, must be viewed in context. There must be no imposition of an "enforced" contemporary presence onto the past, nor a future outlook impressed onto actual circumstances.

Most contemporary landscape studies focus on the interaction of living people with their environment. Ghost research is unique. It also encapsulates the "dead" as "active" presence. What haunts this exchange of temporal presences is a **"structure of feeling" (Williams 1977).** Something is still absent because it is still not completely dead and buried. This "structure of feeling" creates a haunting character that is still in the process of becoming something more.

In that sense of feeling, Gettysburg is not haunted ("dead and done"). It is still becoming haunted! This haunting is a specific type of social interaction with the past in a place that is "teeming" with history, immersion, and remembrances. A haunted Gettysburg is "where" one can see the invisible, hear the past, and think the previously unrecorded and measured past. This is because the first presence that will be perceived and recorded in the future will be the presence that is doing the haunting today!

Do not become too enamored by the actual. Those who make frequent visits to the battlefield (both visitor and investigator) should be aware that the recent past, and the ensuing future, may be different. Gettysburg is still transforming. This transformation goes beyond ecological, man-made, and technological changes. It will be Gettysburg's current social fields of interaction that will make this transformation a future certainty.

It is also the "night" that has altered contemporary Gettysburg. Significant social interactions do not occur in the bars, restaurants, or hotels of the town. It occurs outside on the fields of the National Park Service battlefield. "Ghost hunting" has transformed the battlefield into "shadow" ground. It is hoped that this "fog of war" is not too "shallow" a concept of the battlefield. The field of battle, largely stripped of the horrific images of carnage, is a place where unknown presences lurk in the shadows, behind monuments, in the darkened woods, and in the open (but bloodless) "killing fields".

This is a much too simplistic approach to Gettysburg's haunted character, a place that contains multiple layers of uncertainty. It is time to "brighten" these foreboding shadows. It is time to "illuminate" the spaces "where" the Gettysburg battlefield is haunted. That enlightenment will expose for all to see how the battlefield has become re-haunted, time and again. The haunted character of Gettysburg continues in archaeological time. The remains of the dead are contained in multiple layers of a stratigraphy of memories and experiences.

John Law (2002) states that the telling of stories about something actively help to understand the story. In talking about and investigating the battlefield, the mediated performances themselves (be they text, images, photographs, simulations, measurements, recordings) all contribute to the re-haunting of Gettysburg. There is no action (or description) today that does not affect the future haunted character of the battlefield. Mediations that describe the battlefield as haunted not only affect the present, they also alter the future! Contemporary acts and social practices is "where" the re-haunting of Gettysburg occurs, again and again.

When one views the contemporary Gettysburg battlefield from a horizontal perspective one sees what remains of many different past and contemporary presences from a single point of vision. The observation and sense of these past remains does not require a psychic's ability, nor does it require a "paranormal" explanation. For example, the following photo, taken in 2013, is a view from Devil's Den looking toward Little Round Top and the "Valley of Death". The photo illustrates the nature of Gettysburg's accumulative layers of haunting.

Photo 6: The Palimpsest of the View from Devil's Den

In this photograph, we can view the following:

- Rock formations that are many thousands of years old;
- The 'battlefield rehabilitation", in the area near the former trolley tracks of the 1890's, begun in 2008;
- The parking lot where a mix of old and new autos are parked;
- The tree-lined summit of Little Round Top, a physical presence that existed well before the 1863 battle;
- A paved road that did not exist in 1863;
- The "engaged vision" of a "sharpshooter" from the 1863 battle at Devil's Den, aiming toward the "Valley of Death" and the "Slaughter Pen", a scene that has not changed for perhaps hundreds of years;
- The tower of the New York Monument, on the summit of Little Round Top, erected in the late 19th c.; and
- The woods located on the eastern slope of Little Round Top, where Bushman, in the 1880's, reported the sounds of Indian war hoops, echoing (perhaps) from a battle that was fought there more than a hundred years before the Civil War began.

The photo identifies "still points" (or "excavation" sites) from which to "unearth" the past, and any lingering presences. This photo represents an archaeological vision and imagination to the landscape's possible human interactions/occupations, and natural processes at work in the landscape setting. It also exposes for view some possible haunting uncertainties.

The Devil's Den-"Valley of Death"-"Slaughter Pen"-Little Round Top palimpsest is a series of traces, vestiges, and presences of various pasts and contemporary past, amid the actual. This accumulative landscape has been built-up, layered-over and over again, and haunted and re-haunted through the decades. Sites like this on the battlefield must be "excavated". The haunting scenarios must be unearthed, layer by layer, through contemporary resonating field investigative practices, such as a "ghost excavation".

In 1991, The National Park Service issued a statement of Management which urged the preservation of **"important topographical features of the battlefield"**. It also stressed the preservation of **"cultural landscapes"** that reflected **"pre-battle 1863 rural agricultural environment but includes those superimposed post-battle elements that are necessary for commemoration and visitor understanding of the battle"**.

In effect, it created multiple haunted layers of uncertainty that included pre-Civil War, Civil War, and post-Civil War elements. To each physical detail of this envisioned landscape, The National Park Service created a plan based on K.O.C.O.A. ("Key Areas", "Observation Areas", "Cover and Concealed Areas", "Obstacle Areas", and "Avenues of Approach"). K.O.C.O.A. was the military terrain strategy that was built from multiple sources, and which divided the battlefield into militarily-defined spaces.

Today, the Gettysburg battlefield can be defined as the "ruins" of the "memories" of these K.O.C.O.A. spaces, and what transpired within them. This is a view of a landscape that contains various pasts, each of which has impacted the present through the continuance of material remains that manifest in particular spaces on this battlefield.

The photographic palimpsest shown above illustrates how the past is always present in the landscape. This confirms the "haunted" character of the setting. The present is being "ghosted" by the occurrence of past presences. This "ghosting" must, by necessity, <u>not</u> one past over the other. It must be "excavated", however, layer by layer of haunting uncertainty. The Gettysburg battlefield was once principally "hallowed ground". The soldiers died in battle, were buried, and commemoration began. "Death" went elsewhere, and de-materialized. Much later, Gettysburg became a ghostly landscape. The "dead" returned, and past "life" came back and re-materialized.

Continuous and cyclical contemporary "ghost hunting" practices on the battlefield (and in the town) are the new haunting palimpsest. This new palimpsest is slowly suppressing the past and its "other" presences. Lost through these suppressions will be the presence of Civil War and pre-Civil War hauntings. What remains of those pasts in the future may only be its presence in our imagination. The re-haunting that is "ghost hunting" will continue the transformation of the "Gettysburg Experience" outward to future generations of visitors and investigators.

The occurrence of past presence in contemporary Gettysburg is a series of fields. These fields are associated with various engagements of its battlefield landscape. The landscape is an ensemble, a gathering place for activities, people, and events within a solid mix of various time frames. Processes of decay, fragmentation, accretion, and transformation continue to shape this landscape. Each one further adds to the haunted character of Gettysburg.

Time, as a non-calendrical element of this continuing presence, both passes and does not. Through time, the landscape increasingly becomes more saturated with more uncertainty, and multiple past presences percolate into and out of the landscape. The idea of presence and absence in this percolating landscape becomes irrelevant because what (or "who") may exist at a particular moment in time may be absent during a particular future time. Gettysburg, as a haunted location, in which various immiscible times manifest, is in a constant state of transformation:

"There was a time when time was not succession and transition, but rather the perpetual source of a fixed present in

which all times, past and future, were contained" (Octavio Paz).

These multiple times, a "ritual" time, is Gettysburg's haunted time. It is not fixed to certain dates (July 1-3), or a certain year (1863). It is not even fixed to a present that contains multiple "still points" of time from multiple pasts. It is, and will always be, what is presently (in "actuality") haunting this landscape. And this haunting is directly tied to present actions. The future of a haunted Gettysburg is contained in these contemporary interactions with these multiple pasts.

Presence remains an arbitrary conjunction of pasts. This status will remain "status quo" because it is based on the actions of others in the here and now. These present actions will affect future manifestations of the past. That is a certainty of these uncertain pasts! In this book, I am interested in how these past material remains may (or may not) be encountered in today's reality of Gettysburg's haunted time. As an archaeologist, I will focus during the 150th Anniversary of the battle on the Civil War presence that may remain from 1863, and not those presences in the intervening years between then (1863) and now (2013).

Photo 7: The "Present" Haunted Time of Gettysburg

B. The Vertical Layers

Past presence at Gettysburg is hauntingly-deep. It penetrates far below the 1863 battle, and contains layers of uncertainty that are also situated above that battlefield layer. The dimensions of the haunting cover multiple and varied historical venues. Memories mark that presence and label the Gettysburg experience as one that is haunted by both the past and the present. Those memories have material and sensory coordinates that are part of the "ruins" of vestiges and traces of presence at Gettysburg. These spaces of presence have their own social biographies, and are linked to cultural sounds, aromas, and sights. Today, the "haunted" memory, however, is largely contemporary, rather than historical.

The Gettysburg landscape is a large storage facility of these past and present memories. The landscape, as a stage of presence, has been at one time or another:

- A Native American and Civil War scene of conflict and death;
- A mass grave site;
- A cemetery;
- A "search" field for missing family and relatives;
- A memory ground for veteran reunions and ceremonial acts of remembrance;
- A massive area for monument location and dedication;
- An amusement park;
- Spaces of legend and folklore;
- A military training site;
- A prisoner of war internment camp;
- A ground for re-enactment;
- A National Heritage Park;

- An unchecked ecological area for flora and fauna growth;
- A landscape that has been modified through "battlefield rehabilitation";
- A "testing" ground for "ghost hunters"; and
- A "phantom" amusement ground for "ghost tourism".

Today, in 2013, at the 150th anniversary of the battle, it is a "ruin" of all these historical, theatrical, and performance fields. This "ruin", buried in layers of uncertainty, is "where" the battlefield is now. This "now" will change in the future, as additional layers of haunting uncertainties are added to the current "hauntscape". Many of the spaces on the National Park Service battlefield, and in the town, contain multiple symmetrical layers of various (and varied) "stages" of presence.

The Gettysburg "hauntscape" has accumulated these multiple occupations of uncertainty and presence throughout its history. Thus, the "ruin" of presence is not in a state of decay. It continues to be built-up through participatory acts that continue to add to (and transform) the haunting patterns that deepen this archaeological "ruin" of a "hauntscape".

The memories of uncertainty are the defining spaces of "excavation" within this "hauntscape". These excavation sites are potentially rich in past and present sensory experiences. Since memory is sensory, the recall of it comes in fragmented vestiges and traces. These are the haunting episodes that are recorded by those who walk this "hauntscape".

The British theatrical director, Peter Brook, states that theatre is a case of "watching". Nothing else is needed, except for the situation in which someone is "watching". If we view the Gettysburg "hauntscape" as a "theatre" of multiple memories, a "watcher" (both present and past) defines the nature of this haunting, marking the surroundings with their <u>own</u> personality, beliefs, and acts. That "watch" becomes a theatrical "ghosting" performance of what was, what is, and what will become part of a Gettysburg experience of its haunting presences.

Spaces and their "watchers" provide the present and future with <u>past</u> memories. Gettysburg, as a place with multiple and varied past "watchers", is a "ruin" that remembers these "watching" moments of presences. They become the "spectators" to the past haunting uncertainties, and they provide the "remains" for the future haunting of the Gettysburg experience. Many of these watchers may be what Augusto Boal (1985) calls a **"spect-actor"**. These are individuals who are co-agents of performance who help to create additional haunting uncertainties.

These Gettysburg memories come from many different sources. When one becomes exposed to a contemporary uncertainty, and not familiar with the behavioral pattern, the "presence" immediately becomes a "ghostly" manifestation. But was it a real "ghost" or a recording of one of the Gettysburg "watchers"? Do we know the difference? These haunting encounters are **"behavioral vortices" (Roach 1996)**, not paranormal vortexes!

The "excavation" of these "behavioral vortices" becomes an archaeological process, not a "ghost hunt". We must peel away and separate the layers. We do this through the identification and exploration (as a non-evasive "excavation") of these multiple layers of individual memory biographies of those (present and past) who have experienced this Gettysburg "hauntscape".

The Civil War battle of 1863 was the central event of the region's contemporary presence. It cannot be easily separated from what was there (as presence) before, or what came after. In both instances (a more remote past/post-battle future), many memories are erased and/or suppressed by the destructive impact of the 1863 battle (and its remembrances) on these memories. Today, through ghost tourism and ghost hunting, the focus remains on the continuing presence of the Civil War. The cost of this concentration is the loss of other layers of haunting uncertainties.

A means must be designed to make a space for, and allow other presences to emerge, these haunting memories of the present and past. Only then can we fully begin to understand the historical significance of the "Gettysburg Experience". Today, we need different methods for documenting the multiple and varied historical and contemporary haunting presences of Gettysburg, and transforming these presences to public knowledge.

The re-built and "re-habilitated" battlefield and monumental space plan has to be modified from merely becoming a fossilized memory of Civil War presence. Ghost tourism has to become more of a living epitaph upon which concerned citizens can document and record the flux, flow, and depth of the haunted layers of this Gettysburg experience. And the concept of "ghost hunting", with its emphasis on entertainment, "demand and command" mentality, and its exploitative focus on <u>contemporary</u> concerns, must stop!

Today, what has happened in Gettysburg in the past 30 years is clearly stated in an article by Eelco Runia (2006):

"the past may have a presence that is so powerful that it can use us, humans, as its materials".

This is the problem of viewing the Gettysburg experience as merely a Civil War battle, the military event, and not a culturally-constructed locale of different haunting fields through history. The Gettysburg "ghost soldier" is a metonymy of Gettysburg's history: material remains from the past (perceived as the ghostly presence of soldiers) stands for, almost exclusively, that past as a reflection, however fleeting, of Gettysburg history. Has this created a phantom image of experience? It is a distorted image and memory of what happened here, or a temporary ghostly presence?

The commonality of many other past silences reflected this restricted image of Gettysburg history. Silence is not absent. Presences from the past (multiple pasts) are all around this landscape, seen if one merely "looks"! Some important questions to consider are these:

- Can a revolving experience produce a haunting presence <u>without</u> producing myths (a perceived ghostly presence)?
- Has the National Park Service "rehabilitation program" changed <u>more</u> than the Civil War landscape? Has it altered earlier past presences in the area?
- How does a Civil War haunting presence affect daily observations and experiences in Gettysburg?
- What really happens when we make (or alter) a particular past a "ritual pilgrimage" to Gettysburg (such as the ghost tours and "hunts" for Civil War presence)? Does the divide between subjectivity and objectivity become blurred?

The end result of all these questions may be that a well-rounded "Gettysburg Experience" may be an unattainable goal? In many cases, a perceived presence (such as a "ghost soldier") becomes a poetic encounter. It haunts because the encounter was uncanny: a mystical, philosophical meeting that is a mixture of surprise, amazement, and the knowledge that something horrific really happened there. This creates what Alfredo Gonzales-Rubio has called an **"empty place in a forest full of ghosts"**. Is this the real reality, the totality of the "Gettysburg Experience" in the 21st century?

The history of a landscape is more than the biography of a town or the narrative of a great battle. It is a powerful tool to bring the dead and forgotten moments (from multiple pasts) back to haunt the living by their continued relevance today in memory and embodiment. This is more than a place memory, or a "ghost" of a particular event and situation. It is the history of multiple, and different, peoples who have lived, worked, and inhabited this landscape we call today "Gettysburg".

The Gettysburg experience is more (much more) than a haunted Civil War battlefield. It must become a field laboratory where extensive ghost research can be executed. This research must focus on the unearthing, layer by layer, the haunted character of the accumulative cultural Gettysburg landscape. Through these "excavations", we can locate the "where" of the "Gettysburg Experience"!

The Existing Datum of Experience

The critical question one must ask about the "Gettysburg Experience" (and haunted sites in general) is the trustworthiness of the observations and recordings of the experiences with what is left of the multiple pasts of the town and the National Park Service battlefield grounds. In order to meet a criterion of trustworthiness, these experiences need to contain at least three elements. These are:

- **Credibility:** This is the basis for comparative analysis, and allows one to determine authentic instances, independently-observed, of the remains of the past at Gettysburg.

Photos 8/9: Which of these Photos Represent a Credible "Remains" of the Past?

Photo 9:

- **Dependibility:** The experience of the encounter with the past must meet the criteria of "auditability": the observer/recorder must provide a sufficiently clear and logical account of the encounter which allows investigators to follow the observer/recorder's thinking and conclusions concerning the phenomena, and/or duplicate the results.

- **Transferability:** The observation, recording, or measurement conforms to past context that goes beyond the immediate situation and physical space. The data is sufficient (and credible) which enables the individual (and others) to access its relation to a situation and/or cultural expression from the past.

Photo 10/11: Are these Images of 1863 Seen Today on the Gettysburg Battlefield?

A major problem (and concern) with the existing "Gettysburg Experience" as a past presence authentic encounter (as opposed to a "staged authentic" encounter) is the lack of one or more of these criteria. In general, the majority of "experiences" is not credible for comparative purposes (present to past cultural situation). Most experiences are based on "staged" presentations and/or are subjective, emotional accounts of experiences that were not conducted under controlled conditions, and/or did not accurately portray the accounts in the historical record. Specifically, I perceive a number of problems with the current probability of encountering a real past presence of remains at Gettysburg. These include:

- Regarding the Civil War presence, many fieldworkers (not only "ghost hunters") do not take into account the I.M.P. behaviors of the "culture of war" of the American Civil War. This historical record is vital in identifying the cultural values of the participants, and accounting for their patterned haunting behavior. These would include specific reasons (such as the concept of the "Good Death") why certain individuals might not have wanted to "cross-over" after their death. Another important factor is the particular haunting spaces on the battlefield. How many reports take account of the important relation between a particular haunting manifestation and battlefield military space (the K.O.C.O.A.)?

- Many who have experienced what they thought was a manifestation of past presence have not taken into account the processes of stratification on the battlefield. Traces and vestiges of all past occupations occur on the battlefield, with the latest suppressing the earlier layers. Which layer of uncertainty is manifesting or present at any particular time is unknown, without knowing (or performing) the historical or cultural context of a particular past occupational layer.

- The "Gettysburg Experience" is characterized by different types of reported phenomena that come from a variety of mediated sources, levels of observational experience, and field investigative abilities. Still, the data is integrated and represented in the media as recycled genealogies of common "Gettysburg Ghost Stories", one of the most important themes in the contemporary "Gettysburg Experience".

- There is a paucity of data and experiences with encounters of the "other" layers of historical and cultural occupations in the "Gettysburg Experience". There is a need to document these "others", as it would help to define the haunted landscape.

- There is no clear distinction between "staged" and "authentic" past presence, reenactment and reality, or residual recordings and interactive "apparitional experience". And there is no distinction between "apparitional" appearances of the "living" and those of the "dead".

- There is a lack of controlled and contextual fieldwork. This is largely the result of the proliferation of "ghost hunting" groups and "ghost tourism" operators in the town, as well as the selling of "ghostly" merchandise in many of the local shops. The mythology of the "Gettysburg Ghost" is acted-out nightly in the form of ritualized performances (ghost tours) and participatory overnight tour/investigation packages. These activities reinforce the subjective nature of presence, marketing the "evidence" through internet chat and other media outlets. This "raising the dead", like the "zombie walks", kills the image of ghost research, as performed by serious investigators. It brings entertainment where constructive research should come into play.

- The birth and annual "rite of passage" of the Gettysburg Ghost Conference", characterized by exaggerated egotism, and the fan-based "para-celebrity" event. This is pure entertainment, and has nothing to do with legitimate research, or an authentic "Gettysburg Experience".

In today's reality, the "Gettysburg Experience" has become a highly profitable exhibition of "ghostliness", rather than a true haunting experience with the remains of various pasts. Both the "ghost heritage" (rather than "cultural heritage") and the tourism that supports it, have become symmetrically intertwined: both deal in the intangibles of an absence of substance, an experience that is dislocated from time, space, and historico-cultural content and context.

These by-products of a "phantom" Gettysburg seek to exploit the original notion that something unique happened here, and still remains. It has morphed, however, into something that merely provides entertainment (which is not bad in itself) to the all-to-willing participant, and huge profits for the promoters. But, at what expense is this achieved? History is compromised, culture is forgotten, and the image of the Gettysburg soldier is altered. He (or she) is now just a "ghost"! This is too steep a price to pay for simple entertainment!

An "Excavation" of the "Gettysburg Experience"

"The historical sense involves a perception, not only of pastness of the past, but of its presence".

- T. S. Eliot

The "Gettysburg Experience" is a palimpsest, a documentary record that has been inscribed, time and again, with the remains of vestiges and traces of previous experiences that remain detectable in the landscape. These material remains form an unfolding symmetry in the physical spaces known today as Gettysburg. Through the years, and the centuries, this symmetry has evolved, creating a mythological world, culminating in what only can be described as a pilgrimage to a sacred shrine (at the same time both historical and paranormal) at the beginning of the 21st century.

The anthropologist, Franz Boas, once described a similar cultural process more than a century ago:

- **"It would seem that mythological worlds have been built up, only to be shattered again, and that new worlds were built from the fragments".** (1898)

The history of experience at Gettysburg is a hauntingly human story of the changing images of the memory of presence, each one forming and adding to the growth of this "Gettysburg Experience". The contemporary basis of this pilgrimage, however, rests squarely on the circumstances of events that occurred in 1863, such that these events, "measured by the sad scars of human tragedy, the losses incurred at Gettysburg dwarf those of any other battle in American history" (Asfar and Thay 2004:182).

This sentiment is also echoed by other contemporary authors:

"Their spirits have proven President Lincoln correct- we will never forget what they did here, where they walked, and why they died" (Belanger 2005:126).

A pilgrimage to Gettysburg is a justified venture because this battlefield has become a shrine to fallen soldiers, some of whom are perceived to still remain. This pilgrimage has become, however, an invalid (and over-emphasized) relationship between history and the paranormal:

"I'd like to believe the majority of specters remain as a phantasmagoric honor guard for this sacred place" (Asfar and Thay 2004:112).

According to Mark Nesbitt's "Ghosts of Gettysburg" video (1995), the battle of Gettysburg was **"fought with as much passion, courage, and conviction as ever recorded in the history of warfare"**. This has created a battlefield that has a **"huge unseen population of tormented souls"**, such that Gettysburg may be **"acre for acre the most haunted place in America"**. As with the multiple perceptions of the Gettysburg landscape, Nesbitt has subsequently altered his perception of "haunted Gettysburg". He now calls Fredericksburg, Virginia **"the most haunted city, per capita in the entire United States"** (www.ghostsofFredericksburg.com. – accessed 5-1-07). This shift in worldviews echoes those comments made by Boas more than a century ago.

Still, the Gettysburg battlefield is seen as a mecca for Civil War paranormal activity, at the expense of multiple other manifestations of the past that exist today in the town and on the battlefield. In this vein, the remarks of anthropologist Loren Eiseley seem appropriate:

- **"There are voices out of nowhere whose only reality lies in the ability to stir the memory of a living person with some fragment of the past....both the dead and the living revolve endlessly about an episode, a place, an event that has already been engulfed in time"** **(1971:229).**

That episode, place, and event was (and still remains) the battle of Gettysburg, that was fought there on 1-3 July, 1863. And "ghosts" have become **"synonymous with Gettysburg" (Belanger 2005:122),** such that **"in the database of our collective psyche, we cannot simply cross-reference 'ghosts' and 'war' without seeing one word at the top of the list: Gettysburg" (Ibid: 119).** This year marks the 150th anniversary of that battle. It is fitting, therefore, that the "Gettysburg Experience" today should revolve around this historical event, even though it suppresses other layers of haunting uncertainty in the multiple pasts of presences at Gettysburg.

Gettysburg is a heritage tourism site because (apart from its historical significance) it is located in a largely rural, non-industrialized setting. This sense of place should be rooted in the local (largely Pennsylvania German) cultural landscape. Its architecture, people, material artifacts, ethnic traditions, and folk stories should be a major presence in the "Gettysburg Experience". Yet, the "structure of feeling" that haunts Gettysburg is contextually very specific. It is largely confined to the events and activities surrounding the Civil War battle (and its immediate aftermath). If Gettysburg is indeed a haunted landscape, why then is the majority of reported hauntings so temporally and spatially-specific: a Civil War battlefield? With respect to cultural and/or ethnic heritage, there is little or no data, and there are minimal folkloric traditions (along occupational, gender, or age groupings) relative to the "Gettysburg Experience".

Where are the pre/post-Civil War experiences of presence that haunt Gettysburg? Where are the presences of women and children (except in a few cases) in the "Gettysburg Experience"? This includes the "ghostly" population of Gettysburg. There are few ghosts arising out of, and operating in, individual haunting uncertainties and/or non-military residual activities (except for the Jennie Wade, "Jeremy", and the Orphanage hauntings). Nor do we see individual physical features providing folkloric or haunting experiences (except for perhaps the lore of Devil's Den).

There isn't much non-human experiences at Gettysburg, giving "human" and "other" qualities of "spookiness" to the woods, water sources, and hills surrounding the town and the fields of battle (except for perhaps Little Round Top, and the "White Lady" manifestations of Spangler's Spring). Where are the stories in the Gettysburg landscape of "demons" (excluding Devil's Den), good and playful "nature spirits" and "elementals", animal spirits, and the haunting uncertainties of certain spaces in the landscape (such as the woods on the eastern slopes of Little Round Top)? This is unusual because there was a Native American presence here, and the German and Pennsylvania Dutch, the largest ethnicities in the area, have rich folklore traditions.

In summary, the contemporary "Gettysburg Experience" is quite limited in scope regarding both history and cultural expression. Is this due to the importance that is given to Civil War history, and the contemporary expressions of presence (such as reenactments, "living history" displays, and ceremonies and events that celebrate the Civil War)? Is the "Gettysburg Experience" really historical, or is it man-made, a business enterprise that controls the flow and distribution of this Gettysburg presence? Visit Gettysburg today, and decide: let your experience of the town and the battlefield spaces provide the outcome!

Summary: The Contemporary Gettysburg Marketing Image

The marketing of the current "Gettysburg Experience" is basically a Civil War experience, with residual and active presences from that period in frequent exposition and manifesting quite frequently on tour circuits. Alternative experiences, though present in the past, have largely been overshadowed today by the contemporary emphasis on Civil War presence.

Photo 12: Contemporary Civil War Presence

Photo 13: Contemporary Civil War Presence

Photo 14: Contemporary Civil War Presence

Photo 15: Contemporary Civil War Presence

This current "Gettysburg Experience" is based on three characteristics. These are:

- **"Spookiness":** Gettysburg today is characterized by large numbers of ghost tours and ghost story merchandizing (books, clothing, exhibits, etc.). There is even a "Ghost Lab". The ghost stories involve a small number of basic themes (the majority of which are battlefield-related), and are circulated throughout various media venues in and around the town. They are also part of a number of "tour packages" at hotels and bed and breakfast in the area. These foster and maintain a Civil War ghost folklore and mythology, independent of local ethnic traditions. The military engagement, described in vivid detail throughout Gettysburg, as the most important (and bloodiest) on American soil, further reinforces the ever-growing aura of a spooky landscape;

- **"Haunting Uncertainties":** Personal accounts, reinforced by tour/ghost hunt packages, and consisting mostly of subjective experiences, add to the "spookiness" of the town's phantom population. These "ghost stories" promote individual (and group) searches for authentic experiences with Gettysburg's "ghost soldiers". Unfortunately, in many instances, any phenomena that cannot readily be explained are treated as "paranormal", and associated with a "haunting". This further adds to the growth of ghost lore, reinforcing Gettysburg's ghostly image. This influences the public demand for "hunting" more of these authentic experiences;

- **"Ghostliness":** Many first-time visitors who experience this "spookiness" and the possibility of a "haunting uncertainty" misinterpret audio-visual manifestations on tours, and on the battlefield, as sounds and images of Civil War origin. This suggestibility factor reinforces the idea of a ghostly presence. This, in turn, lends credence to the same "spookiness" and "haunting uncertainty". The result is an endless, repetitive, cycle of subjectivity, perceptual bias, and reinforced through effective marketing techniques.

The system of "apparitional experience" is self-perpetuating because it is an involuted process. Unfortunately, many current ghost investigations as "hunts" are based on these assumed authentic characteristics of the Gettysburg ghost experience. Let's now examine the "evidence" (or lack thereof) for this current, and popular, "Gettysburg Ghost Experience", considered by many to be the most haunted battlefield in the world.

The Implications of Digging Deep
into Hallowed Ground

The Gettysburg battlefield fulfills many different roles, but one experience: that of Civil War presence, seen, unseen, and felt. It would be a great disservice, however, to the continuing influx of visitors (and their personal interests and beliefs) to emphasize one role or perception over another. Gettysburg is a physical location with a multitude of different and haunting settings, each embodied within its own contextual historical and socio-cultural parameters.

A once-inhabited space, or more accurately, one that <u>remains</u> continually inhabited by both the living and the dead, is a place that includes more than a <u>single</u> negotiation of interactions within that space. At Gettysburg, we have the remains of a Civil War battlefield. That is obvious. But we <u>also</u> had, until recently, unabated natural growth in the landscape. The National Park Service response was "battlefield rehabilitation".

We have the appearance, through decades of re-commemorations, the placement of more than 1300 monuments on the battlefield, and the visitor perceptions of these monuments. There is the constant flow of contemporary presence through battlefield-guided tours, re-enactor events, and (at night) ghost "hunts". All of these actions and re-actions are physical <u>and</u> cultural re-negotiations of that battlefield space. They are specific (and sometimes personal) responses to the perceived and known history of the battlefield.

Because of this multiple battlefield "role-playing", we become embedded to multiple realities on that historic battlefield. Unlike the "ghosts" that are perceived there (and do <u>not</u> change their haunting behavior), the battlefield itself has become a constant source of agentic change. There are a number of elements that represent this change. The knowledge of their significance requires an archaeological sensitivity to culturally haunted space.

On a battlefield, such as Gettysburg, this cultural space is part of the **"culture of war" (Fussell 2008)** of the American Civil War. The elements of change that can change the perception of this "culture of war" include:

- A gathering of individuals or groups for specific purposes and actions;
- Role-playing, re-enactments, cultural performances, and ghost tourism and "investigative hunts" as part of these actions; and
- An embedded "archive" of residual and/or interactive recordings/manifestations that are the result of these many transactions and interactions.

The historical past, the contemporary past, and the actual (the present moment) all compete for time, space, and perception in this percolating environment. This can (and has) lead (led) to much confusion and disorientation of what actually is perceived and experienced. Was that manifestation, that sense of presence, something or someone from the historical past, the contemporary past of a few years ago, or someone presently walking the battlefield and alive (not dead)?

The result is a matrix of associations, those between competing presences, and those of competing perceptions of those presences. This matrix differs for each area of haunted space on the battlefield, and for the individual or group (with their own set of beliefs and agendas). This is because these spaces, and those individuals, are composed of personal experiences and memories, both historic and contemporary. And each one is uniquely human.

An understanding of presence on the battlefield must involve an "excavation" that is relative to the characteristics of specific haunted spaces on a Civil War battlefield. A constructive baseline for this "excavation" begins by dividing the Civil War battlefield into five categories where combat and death were experienced in 1863. This positional framing consists of the following military spaces, containing the historic "culture of war" behaviors, the Inherent Military Probabilities (I.M.P.), or what the soldier would have experienced in particular situations:

- **Key Terrain:** This includes those physical spaces that were seized, retained, or controlled during the battle. This terrain is the objective of the military campaign. It's location is rife with haunting uncertainties;

- **Observation Areas:** These areas include signal stations and areas that commanded a panoramic view of key areas of the battlefield terrain. These areas have less haunting uncertainties;

- **Cover and Concealment Areas:** These include stone walls, wooded areas, ridges, large rocky outcrops, and other physical features that offered physical protection from rifle and cannon fire. These areas are depositories of residual elements (such as a soldier's memories of family and "home");

- **Obstacle Areas:** These include wooden fences, buildings, field fortifications and palisades, and other man-made obstructions that affected the flow and movement of advancing troops toward the key area. These areas would be largely void of haunting uncertainties; and

- **Avenues of Approach:** These are the dirt roadways, the farm lanes, and the open fields where the troops advanced toward the objective, the key area. These would be spaces of considerable residual and interactive presences, largely auditory in nature (since a Civil War battlefield was a soundscape, and not a landscape to those in combat within its spaces).

These five military spaces constitute the **"K.O.C.O.A."**. The "K.O.C.O.A." was the military terrain strategy that was used by both General Robert E. Lee and George Meade at Gettysburg. Today, it is still used at West Point to instruct cadets on the nuances of battlefield movement, tactics, and their relation to the physical environment. The "K.O.C.O.A." is used for positional surveys to locate both residual and interactive memory zones ("haunted" space) on the battlefield. The "K.O.C.O.A." is the site of our "ghost excavations". Each of these battlefield spaces tells a different (and haunting) story of what occurred on the Gettysburg battlefield in 1863.

Within each of these "K.O.C.O.A." spaces, there is also personal or proxemics space. This personal-proxemics space is historic/ethnographic cultural space, the "culture of war" space. This space represents the potential "agency" of a haunting. These are the specific individuals who may be haunting a particular "K.O.C.O.A." space. Each haunting manifestation would be based on that soldier's personal space, itself based on their cultural/ethnic characteristics.

At Gettysburg, these personal spaces would also be defined by the soldier's geographical background (rural or urban setting), affinity (North or South) and occupation (farmer, merchant, professional, etc.). Each of these patterns would be a significant element in any investigative performed practice of a "ghost excavation" within these "K.O.C.O.A." spaces.

The ethnographic space of the "culture of war" should be vertically-defined. They exist beneath a more contemporary occupied (haunted) space. The historical battlefield (and haunted) spaces are located in these specific "K.O.C.O.A." spaces. These "haunted" spaces do <u>not</u> change their spatial positioning through time, though some of the unchecked vegetative growth may "mask" their continuing visual presence.

Symmetrically-mixed within these "K.O.C.O.A." spaces are <u>contemporary</u> horizontal spaces, some of which may <u>also</u> be haunted. These spaces consist of at least four patterns. These include:

- Independent tourist paths, some of which are habitually-used by particular individuals, time and again;
- Defined tour circuitous routes used by the National Park Service Rangers;
- Re-enactor spatial territories that are defined by National Park Service policy; and
- "Ghost hunting" space. These spaces are based on popular Gettysburg ghost books, Gettysburg ghost tourism, word of mouth, and internet paranormal sites.

Each of these elements has differing effects on the contemporary haunting uncertainties of the battlefield. These "effects" have been increasing in scope and degree in the last decade or so. All of these four contemporary elements, however, <u>do</u> suppress previously-layered historical haunted space. The result is a continuous <u>re-haunting</u> of the Gettysburg battlefield.

This means that the previous certainties of an original 1863 historical haunting are becoming <u>less</u> certain as "ghost hunts/tourism" <u>increase</u> on the battlefield. The inauthenticity of the majority of these "hunts" (relative to the 1863 "culture of war") is a major factor in this "cover-up". Since this does not occur in <u>all</u> areas of the original

"K.O.C.O.A." space, the battlefield has become today a checkerboard pattering relative to haunting uncertainties.

On the battlefield, at any given time, the landscape (as a 1863 battlefield "soundscape") is percolating with potential presences and absences, altering the current haunting certainties in which to experience the Civil War. A "ghost excavation" brings a semblance of order to this percolating landscape through the use of contextual performances of the "culture of war" in specific battlefield "K.O.C.O.A." spaces. We use contextual "soundmarks" (bugle calls, drum rolls, the Confederate "Yell", period music, etc.) to "excavate" the remains of 1863 presence.

These investigative performances allow us to unfold time through cultural resonance. Without controlled order and investigative strategy in place, an "investigation" becomes merely a "ghost hunt" for something that is, for the most part, a hit or miss endeavor. A "ghost excavation" allows for multiple manifestations of the presence of this 1863 "culture of war". The archaeological sensitivity to "unearth" a particular layer of presence through a controlled process (the 'ghost excavation') allows us to identity particular individuals, manifesting as that haunting presence.

The "ghost excavation" is one controlled and focused negotiation of the many layers of haunting uncertainty at Gettysburg, all of which modify (to different degrees) the battlefield. The common (and symbolic) theme of "acre for acre the most haunted battlefield" is a very limiting concept. Gettysburg is haunted, and is still being haunted. This haunting process will continue into the future, changing our perceptions of how it is haunted today.

We cannot, however, be oblivious to other possibilities, and the importance of contemporary (non-1863) presence. We will always deal with haunting uncertainties in the plural sense. This opens for us a far greater empirical realm to work with than a mere "ghost hunt".

A "ghost excavation" recognizes how risky and how difficult it is to assume and maintain an enduring, haunted past. Archaeological excavations have proven that change occurs all the time. It has also shown us that many of those changes have led to cultural extinction. That truly is a haunting thought, a moment of contemplation we should consider when we investigate Gettysburg's haunted past. There is an increased possibility that the historical past of Gettysburg, which remains as vestiges and traces of presence, will become permanently effaced through non-contextual (and non-resonating) "ghost hunt entertainment"!

The "Black Holes" of Spectral Gettysburg

If the contemporary "Gettysburg Experience" is a ghostly one, centered on the Civil War battle, then this spectrality is lacking in much information pertaining to the history that justifies the haunting! If the battlefield is haunted by Civil War soldiers, shouldn't the past that exists in the present be the one that these same "ghost soldiers" knew? Shouldn't we <u>also</u> know (through their manifestations) the real cultural performances of battle, the Inherent Military Probability (I.M.P.) behaviors of the "culture of war" of the American Civil War?

"Any soldier at Gettysburg knew more about the battle than I do now, even without having any idea of what units were where or who else was doing what" (Gramm 1994:119).

Gettysburg's historic battle has a number of **"black holes" (Frassanito 1995:325).** These are battlefield areas where there is an absence of data concerning the performances of particular military units. One of these "black holes" is the area where the 10th, 15th, and 53rd Georgia (Semmes and Bennings Brigade of McLaws Division), and Kershaw's 15th South Carolina fought at the Rose Farm site. We have (to date) no information on what they experienced in that intense engagement. This being the case, how can we measure and interpret any manifestations coming from this battlefield space today, without referencing and comparing the contemporary experience to that of these men in 1863? We cannot!

We know the end result of what happened to some of these men. They died. But we do not know what they <u>experienced</u>, so we cannot experience, record, or measure what really haunts this place. This makes these soldiers "phantoms", not "ghosts" of a Gettysburg <u>past</u> experience.

"The Rose Farm is a grave....I heard nothing except for bits of sound (of a Civil War scholar's explanation to tourists gathered there) from across that grave where rows of bodies lay....." (Gramm 1994:148).

These were contemporary voices of the "living", not the "dead". How can we authenticate an EVP here, its historical accuracy, if we do not know what these men experienced......not one? We cannot! And this is just <u>one</u> example of a battlefield "black hole". How many more EVP's become "in-authenticated" because of these "black holes". These EVP's cannot be verified as "authentic" because we do not have the historical record to authenticate these as "experienced" voices of particular engagements and military units of the battle.

It is important to note that the existence of these "black holes" (that occur throughout the battlefield) is ignored by many "ghost hunters", who merely scan their audio recorders (or "ghost boxes") in search of "spirit voices". Without the historical record, these "voices" are useless as relevant data. An EVP, under these circumstances, creates more "black holes"! This does not authenticate the research. It creates an <u>alternative </u>reality, one that cannot be based on the historical record. They become part of the mythology of a haunted battlefield!

"Everything that one has ever created achieves reality.....one finds oneself at the mercy of the reality that one has created" (Laxness 1997:35).

Most "ghost hunts" are entertainment, not serious research. They "entertain" a perception of ghosts, not real past presence. If one wants to have a "Gettysburg Experience" that involves authentic Civil War presences, do not, I repeat, <u>do</u> <u>not</u> go "ghost hunting"!

The Gettysburg Battlefield: The Multiple Absence of Presence

The ghosts of Gettysburg are perceived (literally) as "phantom" images. There is little or no distinction made in the ghost lore between the "colors" of the Civil War: "Blue" or "Grey". There has not been, since ghosts were first perceived and conceptualized on the battlefield, a comparative study of how many Union and Confederate ghosts there are at Gettysburg, and that comparison compared to the number of battlefield dead. Why? It is because the documentation of ghosts at Gettysburg is merely a "hunt" for an experience, and not a scientific investigation of the actual "remains" of past presence?

Should we, however, make a ghostly distinction between Union and Confederate ghosts? If there is documented presence of ghosts, why not document their affiliations as well? If one believes the hype and lore that Confederate soldiers, dying a long distance from home and lying today in unmarked graves creates haunting uncertainties, then the ghosts of Gettysburg Confederates should outnumber those of Union ghosts. And if we take into consideration the ritual of the "Good Death", dying at home surrounded by family, burial in the family plot, and with the proper rituals, those Confederates (and Union) soldiers who died and were hastily buried on the battlefield should manifest today as Gettysburg ghosts. Where are these, perhaps multitudes, of Confederate ghosts? Can one distinguish a difference between an "apparitional experience" in relation to a manifesting Confederate ghost, as opposed to a Union ghost? If exhaustive historical research is done, I propose, this distinction can be made.

Do distinctions occur between a "ghost officer" (Union or Confederate) and a "ghost soldier"? Are their differences in frequency and type of manifesting past presence? Does it matter? Is experience more important than documentation? Should we document the "living dead" as thoroughly as the battlefield dead were recorded in 1863? Did the lack of proper documentation in 1863 (such as the scores of "unknown" grave sites of many of these soldiers) result in Gettysburg ghosts? Does the lack of a contemporary and controlled documentation of battlefield ghosts change or nullify the nature of this "hallowed ground"? These are important questions to consider <u>beyond</u> coming to Gettysburg for that "haunting" Civil War "Gettysburg Experience"!

Are the Gettysburg ghosts <u>just</u> human? What about the number of dead animals that were killed on the battlefield? There were about 4,000 of them. Do we count them as Civil War ghosts? Do we even have manifestations of "horse ghosts" on the battlefield? Or, do we have manifestations of a complex haunting there: horse and soldier?

Photo 16A & 16B: Dead Horses on the Trostle Farm

Photo 16B:

One of the first haunting experiences that I had on the battlefield, decades ago, was at the Trostle Farm. As I was walking that part of the battlefield, I suddenly perceived this overwhelming stench of blood and decaying flesh. At the time, I did not know about the Trostle Farm horse slaughter. Afterwards, visiting a local bookstore, I saw a book of Gettysburg battlefield photos, and a photo of the dead horses on the Trostle Farm. The barn structure was the key piece of identification, as I recalled that it was in that precise area that I sensed that overwhelming smell of decaying flesh. Was this a residual of those dead horses? Perhaps......

Horse and carriage hauntings (as residual elements) were common manifestations in England, before the Industrial Revolution. Gettysburg, before and during the Civil War, was noted for its cart, wagon, and carriage industries. The story of the "Jeremy" haunting on Baltimore Street is an example of a haunting associated with horses and carriage. These industries totaled 15 business establishments in the town prior to the Civil War. Did I perceive a pre-Civil War residual haunting prior to the battle of 1863 or what occurred there on July 2, 1863? I don't know, but the uncertainty helped to re-define my investigative methodology of layered "ghost excavations".

If the Gettysburg "ghosts" included animal as well as human dead, would it detract from the socio-cultural and spiritual beliefs of mid-19th century Americans? Would the image and significance of fallen soldiers on the battlefield change, such that:

"not only do these actions dishonor the slain by treating them more like animals that humans; they diminished the living who found themselves abandoning commitments and principles that had helped them to define their essential selves" (Faust 2008:100).

Do human and horse ghosts that manifest on the battlefield alter our perception of the afterlife, or what it means to <u>become</u> a "ghost"? Perhaps........and how does this uncertainty affect our experience of the Civil War at Gettysburg?

The burial sites of horses are indicated on the "Elliot Map", drawn-up around the middle of July 1863 by S. G. Elliot of Philadelphia. Portions of this map are illustrated in Gregory A. Coco's book on Gettysburg (1995). One specific location where "ghost horses" might be encountered would be the Trostle farmhouse. According to William T. Livermore, a volunteer in the 20th Maine:

"Caisons stood where the horses were instantly killed by a cannon ball and they piled up on the pole just as they were

killed…..19 horses lay in the bigness of…(the) barnyard" (quoted in Coco 1995:50).

Should investigations be conducted at this (and other) animal "fields of death"? Should these types of investigations be part of the "Gettysburg (Civil War) Experience"? That is an individual decision……..

Photo 17: The Trostle Farm today

If we have a large number of animals haunting the battlefield, how does this affect the concept of "hallowed ground"? If "hallowed ground" is about the sacrifice of human life, what about the sacrifice of innocent animals? Should we consider the human element, or the humane one? If there were an estimated 1.5 million horses and mules killed in the war, how does one define a "haunted" location, if there are manifestations of animal ghosts?

A "ghost" is a dead, once-living subject. It is <u>not</u> an anomaly of a physical object. This question of "ghosts" goes beyond a soul-searching or soul-specific query. It is about the appearance of something that is known to have died, had once lived (as is <u>not</u> an "elemental" or "demon"), and is now manifesting in some sensory form, after physical death. A "ghost" is a "ghost". If there are no animal "ghosts" on the battlefield, then there may <u>not</u> be human "ghosts" as well. You <u>must</u> have it <u>both</u> ways.

The Uniform(ity) of the
Gettysburg Battlefield Ghost

If one is to believe than an individual (or his/her personality) does survive death, then we must <u>also</u> believe that their memories and habits also survive, in the <u>same</u> situation and circumstance as one experienced during life. A "ghost soldier" was a soldier in life. Those soldiers were "uniformed" military men and women. Their "clothed" appearances, therefore, must come from habit and "actual" wear. This was part of regulated conduct and behavior during their lives as Union and Confederate soldiers.

According to the ghost lore, largely unconfirmed, after death there <u>is</u> a change in those individuals who remain as "ghosts". Besides the transformation from a normally-visible state of being to largely an absent presence, there is also a transformation in <u>what</u> remains. This usually consists in vestiges and traces of "remains", manifesting as various sensory elements (auditory, tactile, olfactory, visual, etc.). However, this transformation and fragmentation would occur, I propose, <u>without</u> a corresponding change in character or cultural expression. The "ghost culture" that remains would be the culture of the individual at the time of death. For those who fought and died on the Gettysburg battlefield, that would be the "culture of war" of the American Civil War, and its Inherent Military Probability (I.M.P.) behaviors.

"Ghost soldiers", if they exist, wear clothes (and manifest this image through PSI) for the purpose of demonstrating that they are <u>still</u> soldiers. A "ghost soldier" would <u>also</u> want to be identified with that status, and that period in history in which he lived and experienced life. If these "soldiers" manifest as "ghosts" on the Gettysburg battlefield, they are communicating that experience of war today.

It would be contrary to simple common sense (if we believe that they exist) that "ghost soldiers" would appear in a guise other than "uniformed" military men. The question becomes this: do the "ghost soldiers" on the Gettysburg battlefield appear in their "battle" clothes, and is this appearance being experienced by contemporary individuals on that battlefield?

Are those individuals ("ghost hunter" or casual visitor) who have personally reported experiencing a Gettysburg ghost actually seeing a real dead soldier from the 1863 battle? Or, are they experiencing a residual of a reenactment, and a "sanitized" re-enactor version of what the 1863 soldier must have looked like during the battle? The "uniform" worn during battle was certainly not the clean, bloodless, and odorless clothing of the Gettysburg soldier. What do these perceived "ghost soldiers" look like in their "battle" uniforms?

Furthermore, if the real Confederate soldiers of 1863 had no specific colored, "standard" uniform, how can a casual contemporary observer know "who" is really being "seen" (perhaps for an instant) on the battlefield? Are there clearly-defined criteria that would "authenticate" a Confederate "ghost soldier" of 1863? The largely subjective encounters with "uniformed" ghosts may be merely a contemporary mixture of different sets of reality:

- There may be sightings of some ghost hunter's fragmented version of a Civil War uniform that is being used as a "prop"; or
- It may be a tourist or history enthusiast who has "rented" a uniform for the day at one of the several shops in Gettysburg catering to these individuals; or
- We have a re-enactor's presentation of "authenticity", a uniform precise in every detail, except for one perhaps. If he is wearing a comfortable pair of brogans, how "authentic"

was that for 1863? Many soldiers were "bare-footed", and that was how they fought and died.

Have any of these "phantom" soldiers been seen on the battlefield, and mistaken for "ghost soldiers"? The "uniformity" of the ghost sightings on the battlefield, orderly and relatively "clean", defeats the validity of their authenticity. Real battle-experienced soldiers, as "ghosts", would not be wearing the uniforms that people perceive today as "ghostly".

"Cross-dressing" individuals (present to past; women dressed as "soldiers") may be the key to the hauntings that are observed on the battlefield. If people "see" battlefield ghosts as quite similar to themselves (as "uniformed" representatives), then the "ghost" which they observe (passive, unemotional, without any obvious injury, and a uniform lacking blood, dust, dirt, and odors) becomes a "mirror" image of themselves. It complements the "uniform of the day".

The contemporary versions of the uniform (in reenactments, casual walkers, and ghost hunting "triggers") are not the authentic manifestations from an 1863 battlefield environment. Rather, they are the "imagineerings" of individuals who have little or no contextual understanding of mid-19th c Civil War battlefield experience, and real combat experience!

Photos 18A & 18B: Do These Uniformed Men Attract Civil War Ghosts and/or are Perceived as Ghosts on the Battlefield?

An "Orb" By Any Other Name
is NOT a "Ghost Soldier"!

Note:

This is not a discussion about "dust", "dew", "insects", "camera trappings", or the "human finger".

If a "ghost" includes the "afterlife consciousness" of a past cultural being, then these "ghosts" are not "orbs"! The anomalies that orb(it) around the Gettysburg battlefield, and recorded on film and in photographs, are not the "ghosts" of dead Civil War soldiers.

Marc Auge (1995) has written about the concept of "things", calling some of these, "non-things", something that acts as a backdrop. These "non-things" provide a setting, but have little meaningful associations. "Orbs" are like that. They act as a backdrop for symbolically representing, to many "ghost hunters", the cultural behavior and the acts of a Civil War soldier. Their documentation offers little in the way of advancing the field of ghost research.

There is both a space and time "forgetfulness" to a focus on "orbs" as the documentation of a haunting. Still, their manifestations litter the web pages of ghost hunters, on TV shows like "My Ghost Story", and on "ghost hunts". Yet, an "orb" as a "thing" is an incredibly generalized concept, its meaning is nameless as a thing, and it merely exists for us as "something", not "someone" in particular. The "orb" is a containing element of something, defined in a certain way, and exists for but the shortness of a temporal moment. Is this how we want to define our Gettysburg "ghost soldier"? I think not! The "orb", as a past presence, is not "someone"!

An "orb" is not even an "object" because it is not relatively stable in form. So why is it an object of study, of thought and consideration, or an object(ive) interpretation of a haunting on a Civil War battlefield? The problem: how do we compare an "orb" to a human presence performing a past cultural act of a Civil War soldier?

To have relevance as meaningful data, the "orb" needs to be situated within a cultural context that explores the "orb's" existence as part of the "culture of war" of the American Civil War. Specifically, the "orb" (or other light anomaly) must enact Inherent Military Probability (I.M.P.), or how a soldier would have reacted in a particular military situation. If the "orb" has no I.M.P. context, it remains a "thing", not an interactive past presence ("ghost soldier").

Photo 19: Is this "Orb" Performing an Act of I.M.P. Behavior?

Photo 20: What is the military significance of these "orbs"?

In this sense, to make sense, the focus must be on the way in which a "thing" ("orb") gathers human qualities, linking it together, for a moment, to a soldier's behavior in a specific space on the battlefield. If this linkage cannot be made, then the "orb" is non-representative of anything, and becomes irrelevant: the "orb" is <u>not</u> a "ghost soldier"!

We cannot declare a "ghost soldier" appearance without confirming the patterns that must be left by continuing human behavior. The impact of an event as significant as the Civil War battle at Gettysburg should be observable in the behavioral patterns discovered during controlled, contextual fieldwork on the battlefield. No matter how fragmented the vestiges and traces are that remain, they must account (and become accountable) for (as) a Civil War presence, and <u>not</u> as "anomalies" of a perceived paranormal event.

Every piece (or artifact) of contextual data is precious, needed, and most welcome. The subject of past presence must be studied from multiple viewpoints. To ignore any remains is to create a false image, something we cannot tolerate. All data remains significant, until proven otherwise as redundant. Serious and dedicated fieldworkers must make this determination. It must not be left to others, less noble (more focused on the thrill of the "hunt" or its prospective "entertainment" value), to discover or dismiss this past presence. Only a clear devotion to method and principles can determine if the data has value and contributes to our understanding of a Civil War presence at Gettysburg.

With regard to this specific military presence at Gettysburg, it must not be overlooked, out of some compassionate longing or desire to encounter real "ghosts" on the battlefield, that military sites were created as a result of actions that occurred within a closed cultural system that operated under strict rules and protocols (the "culture of war").

The experiences of individuals (or groups) today on the battlefield concerning perceived manifestations of past Civil War presence must realize that any perceptions of presence, that lie outside this closed cultural system, are not real experiences of Civil War "ghost soldiers". There are many examples of this non-military battlefield behavior that have been reported in Gettysburg ghost books, on ghost tours, during ghost hunts, and on TV shows. To cite a few, these include:

- "Drilling" on the battlefield, especially in battlefield spaces knows as "avenues of approach" toward a military objective;
- The Confederate "tour guide" of Devil's Den who instructs tourists where to take photographs; and

- "Hitchhiking" Civil War soldiers perceived on the back of pick-up trucks, etc.

The detection and documentation of military past presence at Gettysburg, and its multiple layers of presence (including Native American, Colonial, post-Civil War, World War I, etc.), requires particular "excavations" under controlled conditions to properly observe and document this military patterning of fields of behaviors and military acts. Control and context can lead to certainty, and such fieldwork is much less likely to be due to random, anomalous behaviors that are not relative to the analysis of battle and military remains at Gettysburg.

One should also be cautious regarding the experiences of re-enactors, and the effects of re-enactment on the manifestation of past presence. At the battle site of Perryville, Kentucky, re-enactments appeared to have masked the historical data which could have been used to interpret the battle there. To understand military presence, behavior, and experiences on a battlefield, we must place our recorded data onto the image of those individuals behind (and in front of) <u>real</u> ammunition, ordinances, and guns!

For the common soldier in battle, the universe shrank. It contained the fields of social behavior (I.M.P.) that formed a context for this universe, this "theatre of war". This "theatre" became a particular sensorium, not a physical setting. It formed a soundscape for the thousands of other I.M.P. behaviors of soldiers who shared that field of battle. That sensorium was an obscured sound-filled setting as described by Haskell who experienced first-hand the Gettysburg battlefield:

"......a million various minor sounds engaged the ear. The projectiles shriek long and sharp. They hiss, they scream, they growl, they sputter; all sounds of life and rage, and each has its

different tone, and all are discordant. Was ever such a chorus of sound heard before"?

This soundscape battlefield was definitely <u>not</u> the presence or experience of a re-enactment where visual presence, not sonic sensitivity, was the order of the day. Again Haskell remarks:

"At this point little could be seen of the enemy, by reason of his cover and the smoke, except the flash of his muskets and his waving flags".

To appreciate a re-enactment, you have to <u>see</u> it. Those soldiers who experienced a real battle heard it! They did not fully see or visualize its ebb and flow.

Today, the battle for presence is once again being fought. The opposing armies this time, however, are the various advocates of <u>different</u> interpretations of the <u>same</u> past. They fight over a <u>particular</u> presence: "who" is present, and "what" lies in <u>their</u> sights. This was certainly not the presence seen and heard during the actual battle of 1863.

Henry Glassie (1977:32) has stated that **"the past is too important to leave to historians. The human reality is too important to leave to novelists".** And "ghosts", as an <u>interpretive</u> past presence, are too important to leave to "ghost hunters"! We must establish a <u>cultural</u> history of the "Gettysburg Civil War Experience", a "ghost culture" of what (and who) remains from the past. This exploration must become a "ghost culture ethnography" of the continuing expressions of past presence that one can encounter there.

"And so good-bye to the war....future years will never know the seething hell and the black infernal background of countless

minor scenes….of the secession war. And it is best they should not. The real war will never get in the books".

- **Walt Whitman**

Is this the real war that remains as a major characteristic of the "Gettysburg Experience", or has this "ghost war" become a part of popular culture today as a "ghost hunt" on the Gettysburg battlefield? We must analyze the "culture of war" of the American Civil War, and its "normative" aspects, in order to understand what is really manifesting on the battlefield.

A "Normative Ghost Culture"

The "culture of war" of the American Civil War was a "normative" culture. It <u>must</u> have been in order to survive the deadly nature of battle, time and again! If this "normative" culture of war persisted through four years of intense and deadly battlefield engagements, then it also could survive as a social and mental field of memory today, perhaps "triggered" to manifest through resonating acts that mimic those behaviors.

Anthropologist Alexander Lesser (1961:42) uses the term **"social field"** to describe the **"web-like, netlike connections between individuals and their social groups that stretch across time and space"**. If I.M.P. behaviors of the "culture of war" are manifesting on the Gettysburg battlefield in particular militarily-defined spaces (K.O.C.O.A.), then these "social fields" should be perceived and documented by field investigators.

If these "social fields" are **"fields of relationship" (Wolf 1984:397)**, then they should remain and be defined in culturally relevant ways, as I.M.P. behaviors, and not as "orbs", "shadows", or non-contextual battlefield manifestations. In "roll-calls", soldiers should answer, in a contextual way, to their names. E.O.C.'s ("E.V.P.") should reflect this. In areas of intense engagement (like a K.O.C.O.A. "avenue of approach" toward a military objective), we should record the "shouts", "cries", and "struggles" of men (not an individual) in mortal combat. That these <u>do</u> occur is confirmed by our "ghost excavations" at Burnside Bridge (on the Antietam battlefield in Maryland, and on the eastern slopes of Little Round Top on the Gettysburg battlefield). To listen to these recordings, please go to www.ghostexcavation.com.

These I.M.P. behaviors of the Civil War are battlefield sonic signatures. They are ethnographies of communication (E.O.C.) of the "culture of war" of the American Civil War. They are human-human relationships, and human-environment imprints. They must be recorded and perceived as sensory patterns of combat. As the battlefield was foremost a soundscape, these sensory patterns should be largely auditory in character.

What is important in this concept of a "normative ghost culture" of the "culture of war" of the American Civil War at Gettysburg is that this culture (both past and its present manifesting forms) is bound together by common and distinct sets of norms, **"the normative view of culture" (Willey and Phillips 1958:18).** This involves patterns of behavior common to a group, imposed by society upon its members.

This patterned behavior would contain rigid standards or norms of behavior. This is especially appropriate for a military culture. It would include rigid standards of I.M.P. behaviors on a battlefield, such as Gettysburg. This behavioral pattern was achieved in drills, and reinforced in companies, as units of fighting men who knew each other, and who joined the army together from the same geographical area.

On a battlefield, this ordered pattern was critical to successful military operations. I propose that this pattern of I.M.P. behaviors survive as social and mental fields that manifest today, in some cases as vestiges and traces on a Civil War battlefield. It is this precise pattern of social and mental fields that we must document, as examples of an afterlife conscious mind that survives physical death. These social and mental fields are not "floating orbs"!

The concept of a "normative culture of war", consisting of particular I.M.P. behaviors in specific battlefield spaces (K.O.C.O.A.), implies that they must be studied as whole entities, since they are naturally homogeneous. Haunting manifestations of this "culture of war" on the battlefield, however, are not complete images of that culture (and its cultural and mental fields). They will manifest as vestiges ("residuals") and traces ("interactive") of presence as a Civil War "Gettysburg (Apparitional) Experience". These manifestations become the contemporary "ghost culture" of the Civil War.

This Gettysburg-experienced Civil War "ghost culture" is, if properly carried out in fieldwork performance "excavations", defines a particular time and space of past experience, and one recognizable by its cultural expressions of I.M.P. behaviors. The primary objective of fieldwork is not a "hunt" for a Civil War experience, but rather a study of the relationships of haunting forms that are relative to these I.M.P. behaviors of the "culture of war" of the American Civil War, as they would have occurred in particular military spaces at Gettysburg. This becomes a **"cultural archaeology"** of Gettysburg Civil War experience.

The "Gettysburg Experience" of this Civil War "ghost culture" represents, to again reiterate, just one layer of potentially-multiple haunting uncertainties in the Gettysburg landscape. This layered acknowledgement is needed on practical grounds. It effectively reduces the variety of human behavior and occupations on this landscape to a manageable and logistical proportion of one layer at a time, for a controlled scientific analysis and evaluation.

The archaeological record of these manifestations would not be the "culture of war" itself, but rather its cultural product: the materially (sensorially)-expressed norms of the culture that produced it. On a Civil War battlefield, these norms could be sonic recordings of various ethnographies of communication (E.O.C.), involving vocal expressions that reflect these I.M.P. behaviors.

For example, on the eastern slopes of Little Round Top along the 15th Alabama line of attack (an "avenue of approach" in K.O.C.O.A.), we have recorded the voices of soldiers, from Company G of the 15th Alabama, responding to our "roll-call". Not many responded, but <u>some</u> did. Afterwards, portraying Colonel William Oates the commander of the 15th Alabama, I ordered a charge along this avenue of approach toward the embedded positions that the 20th Maine occupied on July 2, 1863.

While simulating this charge, one of the investigators was literally thrown to the ground. We had photographed a "handprint" on the back of the investigator, perhaps indicating that there was a physical presence that caused this. No one visible was near this investigator at the time of the incident. Did a "soldier" do this, perhaps as a means to protect him? We don't know the answer to that uncertainty.

The analysis of the "Gettysburg Experience", as a connection to the Civil War battle and its combatants, was viewed from a perspective of various perceptual constructs: historical time (July 1863); geographical space (battlefield K.O.C.O.A.); social situation (war/combat) and past presence (I.M.P. behaviors of the "culture of war" of the American Civil War).

These constructs, as indicators of presence, rejected instrumental causality ("ghost tech" measurements), geophysical factors (high EMF), and psycho-social profiles (belief; "ghost hunting" mentality: confirmation bias). Instead, there is a focus on people that may <u>become</u> "ghosts", and who represent <u>their</u> worlds through memory practices. These memory practices are based on the socialization processes they created in drills and exhibited, time and again, on the battlefield. It also included the importance of recognizing the manifestation of particular battlefield behaviors (I.M.P.) through the recognition of space as a soundscape and the auditory cues that were necessary to initiate military acts.

What is important in this analysis, and in the concept of a surviving "normative ghost culture" of the "culture of war" of the American Civil War, is that there should be no variations in the material record of what still remains (as the "ghost culture") from the 1863 battle. Any differences that may manifest are relative to quantity (what manifests) and quality (vestige and trace), and not content (I.M.P. behaviors of the "culture of war").

The "baseline" of the "excavation" of these vestiges and traces of the 1863 experience of war is that the "lives" of past presence are as emotional and horrific as those they had in the past during the battle. This is because those present manifestations are the direct outcome of those past lives and deaths. Only with a secure "identity" and recognition of I.M.P. behaviors of the "culture of war" of the American Civil War can we hope, as serious investigators, to involve a manifestation of this behavior (and not an "anomaly") to any kind of plausible relationship with people of a past period. This is to recognize the manifestations for what they are, and therefore what (and who) they were: the manifestations of I.M.P. behaviors in particular battlefield spaces (K.O.C.O.A.) of the "culture of war").

"Well, whether I ever march home again

To offer my love and a stainless name

Or whether I die at the head of my men,

I'll be true to the end all the same

- **William Gordon McCabe, 1864.**

This "truth" is what maintained that battle line and that combat posture: the I.M.P. behaviors. It is the same truth that we seek in a

Civil War battlefield haunting: the manifestations of these I.M.P. behaviors today as "apparitional experiences".

The "excavation" of this Civil War experience, as performance practices that can "unearth" these I.M.P. behaviors, is an investigative construct that can be used as a <u>direct</u> means to re-establish chains of connection from the Civil War past that secure a contemporary identity of a true "apparitional experience". The use of contextually-sound resonances allows us to make that connection, <u>without</u> failing to adequately respect the past.

This lack of respect for Gettysburg's past, as horrific Civil War history, can be seen in many "ghost hunts" and ghost tours through an ideological imposition of present views, notions, and technologies that treat manifesting presences as "anomalies", "paranormal" events, and (worst of all) as public entertainment! The use of an archaeological sensible and sensitive approach to this Civil War presence can be best described as <u>maintaining</u> these links between past and present.

If past presences of multiple histories at Gettysburg remain as mere fragmented "ruins" of anomalous phenomena, rather than a "normative ghost culture", these pasts will remain forever visualized as broken, disarticulated, and "unknown" presences of the past. Even more so, these pasts (and their presences) become alienated from present reality. A "ghost excavation" (see Sabol 2011) can help to re-animate these "normative ghost cultures" as sensible and sensitive past presence. This <u>is</u> therapeutic work!

The "Good Death"

Today, we struggle to understand what (and "who") may be manifesting on Civil War battlefields. Because we fail to research and learn what does manifest there, and "who" is (was) <u>never</u> there, we experience the battlefield as captives of our own times and beliefs. We are unable to know the past, and its continuing presence today on an individual and personal level. The fault is our <u>own</u> making. We make the "ghosts" because it is us who perceive them on the battlefield.

There is a ritual nature to a haunting (and its experience). It produces (re-produces), time and again, <u>expectable</u> cultural behaviors, if only one thoroughly researchers the site's social and spatial histories. These are <u>not</u> "paranormal" histories. This is <u>not</u> for entertainment purposes, so it <u>requires</u> more than a superficial glance, or an occasional "salute" to history. That we have not learned this yet is our own fault, and is the reason why ghost research, despite increased perceptions and investigative groups, has not advanced toward the real objective: purposeful research and fieldwork!

This concept of rituals of expectant behaviors could provide a key to why some spaces <u>become</u> haunted. In ghost research, we must learn the power of cultural belief, and how it can shape an entire socio-cultural world, and way of life, in history. Such is the case of the "good death", and its specific rituals of expectant behaviors:

- To die at home;
- To be surrounded by family who perform the proper rituals of mourning and remembrance; and
- To be buried in the family plot.

The concept of the "good death" is extremely important for understanding why some hauntings occur on Civil War battlefields. The Civil War battlefield destroyed those familiar rituals of the "good death". It led, I propose, to haunting behaviors on many Civil War battlefields.

"Home" was always on the minds of the soldiers, even before combat. According to Reid Mitchell, in *The Vacant Chair (1995)*:

"Remembering home, dreaming of it, planning for an eventual return to it allowed men to focus on something other than the army and the war….."

This focus on home, combined with a death on the battlefield and subsequent quick burial at an unknown grave site could have led to some of the hauntings that are perceived on the battlefield today.

This importance of home to these soldiers "hit home" to me when we recorded the voice of a "soldier singing" about "home" at the 11th Connecticut monument, near Burnside Bridge on the Antietam battlefield in Maryland. You can hear this singing at www.ghostexcavation.com. Was he singing one of the popular ballads of the time, such as the mournful "Weeping Sad and Lonely"? We don't know for sure.

The concept of the "good death" is also part of the "culture of war" that we must "unearth" as part of the "Gettysburg (Civil War) Experience". It is so important to an understanding of past presence at Gettysburg, where so many men (and their identities) were buried and forgotten in unknown graves. These men did not receive the proper burial or mourning rituals, and were interred far away from home and the family plot. Many are still missing (MIA), even today. Yet, this aspect of the "culture of war" has received sparse (if any) attention from ghost hunters.

Ghost hunting at Gettysburg (and on other Civil War battlefields) involves an approach that largely ignores the beliefs and attitudes of mid-19th c. society. North American theater director, Matthew Goulish, once asked: **"What is culture"?** His own answer: **"The formation of attention"**. Let's pay <u>more</u> attention to this "culture of war", and particularly to the concept of the "good death" in ghost research, and in fieldwork on Civil War battlefields.

Charles A. Fuller, 61st New York, who was wounded at Gettysburg, wrote about how relatives traveled to the battlefield in search of loved ones. Seeing this, he made the following comment:

"It shows what was going on in thousands of families the land over – North and South – and it is the kind of matter that does not get into books on war subjects".

It does, however, get into our strategy of "ghost excavations" on these Civil War battlefields! The concept of the "good death", and the search for missing relatives on the battlefield, has been used very successfully in our "ghost excavation" performance practices at Burnside Bridge, on the Antietam battlefield in Maryland (see Sabol 2011/2013). Beginning in the fall of 2013, we will be applying these same investigative performance practices on the Gettysburg battlefield.

Any interpretation of an uncertain past manifestation is full of difficulties. It is not simply a "ghost" or a "haunting". We project, especially on a ghost tour or "hunt", too much of our own beliefs (and prejudices) back into the past. On the Gettysburg battlefield, is one really perceiving the experience that haunted the soldier on the battlefield? And I am <u>not</u> talking about "seeing the elephant" (Civil War battle).

That lingering question, still not answered, is why, I believe we will never be sure of what we experience there until we understand and become aware of what these soldiers believed about life, the "good death", and what it meant to die far from home and family. If we do not (or cannot) acknowledge this behavior of the "culture of war", our experiences on the battlefield will remain "anomalies", something that is beyond our comprehension of a particular culture at war.

Many of us will never know (or understand) why some of these men still haunt the battlefield. It will remain a mystery to those who don't know the underlying beliefs that motivated some of these soldiers to remain there on the battlefield, even today. This was (and is) a cultural, not a religious, belief towards home and family.

Because of this lack of empathy to their cause, for those on that battlefield today from the past, some of us cannot comprehend why they were willing to offer-up their lives. For these men (those who lived and those who remain), their sacrifice make perfect sense; their remaining there, a perfect example of what a 'good death" meant within their beliefs about the world and the reality that they inhabited. Those beliefs and that reality are not ours. But we can experience it through their memories that haunt us today.

Their sacrifice suggests that this (their battlefield deaths) was no passing fancy, no impulse, and certainly no habit. Rather, it was a deeply-rooted means of understanding life and death. To sense how ingrained those beliefs were (and continue to be), we need to follow them (their beliefs) back in time. To explore that world, however, we must leave far behind the 21st century, and move into their century. We must inhabit that same reality. This is NOT entertainment! This becomes the real experience of the Civil War soldier.

Summary: The "Gettysburg (Civil War) Experience

One walks the surfaces and observes the trenches. This becomes the recognition of presence from a measurement of what remains, and "who" is still lost and forgotten on the battlefield.

Photo 21: What Remains is Still Lost in This Photograph?

Photo 22: What Remains Here?

Presence without memory is no "life" at all. It becomes a "ghost". In ghost research, we must document the presence of past interactive remains, and not the "ghosts of place".

The locations of the remains of active presence, despite centuries of acknowledgement, remain a haunted setting, one of the greatest unknown lands that remain for all sciences that work with what is left of the past. Is it a question of an afterlife consciousness, or merely a life of unconscious (subjective) perception? The becoming of this presence remains a matter of mystery. We sense that spectral geography at a perceived haunted location, but is that sensation based on a real sense of past presence?

A "ghost excavation" (Sabol 2007.....2013) seeks how a "dig", that explores the uncertainty of becoming (as a continuing cultural being/identity still in place), is a performative process in which past memories play a recurring (and pivotal) role. It is these past memories that must become an integral component of the "Gettysburg Experience" as a Civil War presence.

We must take constructive and directed steps toward a human acoustemology of a haunted battlefield, and not "entertain" a "paranormal" anomalous series of experiences. The memory of battle still remains as a fragmented cultural world of war. Its manifesting embers still retain the experience of "hearing the elephant", a sensate feeling that can burst back into a renewed form of life today on the battlefield. An "afterlife conscious mind" is made-up of these memories, an identity form, and intent for becoming present again.

We must not fall into a ghost hunt mentality which, at best, measures physical degrees/changes. This was not how a battlefield was experienced or fought by Civil War soldiers. The battlefield was not just a particular place. It became a field of meaning through sonic cues, tied to I.M.P. behaviors, memories that were already established by drills as habits.

We must map the spectral geography of Civil War battle, and its social and mental fields of I.M.P. behaviors. This deep acoustical mapping can help to reveal a more precise rendering of the experience of battle that is manifesting today. This is "minding" the past, not re-inventing it, or re-playing it back again today.

The Gettysburg battlefield, viewed in analytical terms as a landscape where a horrific battle was fought, can be measured, located spatially, and data can be analyzed by contemporary instruments. Such work is important, perhaps essential for some investigators. But it does not take the present into the past, nor does it make that past manifest today.

This is because technology involves processes that are time-specific to today, as an approach to contemporary reality. But this does not immerse us into the cultural mind set of I.M.P. behaviors of the "culture of war" of the American Civil War. That immersion should be the goal of all those who come to Gettysburg for a Civil War experience.

At the same time, we must "outlaw" the "usual suspects" of typical ghost hunting measured presence. Are localized geophysical processes the cause of a haunting because of their effect upon the living (hallucination; sensory alteration), or its effect on our perceptions of the appearances of the dead (an indicator of a haunting: high EMF; drop in temperature)? What happens in those cases with very specific manifestations that seem to be products of design, agency, are purposeful, or are of human intelligence relative to specific contextual socio-cultural situations? These manifestations negate the relevance of measured space! We have documented these cultural manifestations during "ghost excavations" <u>without</u> the use of "ghost tech" measurements!

What must survive to be an authentic "apparitional experience"? According to Quinton (1975), it is the

"absolutely minimal embodiment, as when a recurrent and localized voice of a recognizable tone is heard to make publicly audible remarks" (1975:71).

We have recorded, time and again, these "recognizable" and "publicly audible remarks" on Civil War battlefields (you can hear them at www.ghostexcavation.com).

According to Braude (2003), the evidence suggests the following:

"the existence of occurrent mental states belonging to a deceased individual, but also the persistence of dispositional states (memories, traits, attitudes, abilities, etc.)" (2003:294).

This requires

"something that contains (or carries or holds) the disposition and which can eventually express the disposition in occurrent states" (Ibid: 294).

If someone survives physical death, it is

"a series of mental states connected by continuity of character and memory" (Quinton 1975:65).

On Civil War battlefields, we have recorded, during a "ghost excavation", this "continuity of character and memory". We <u>have</u>

recorded the auditory character of I.M.P. behaviors of the "culture of war" of the American Civil War (www.ghostexcavation.com).

This hypothesis of the survival of I.M.P. behaviors as a form of afterlife conscious mind is survival with limited agency: vestiges and traces, sonically-expressed, of the "culture of war" on Civil War battlefields. According to Griffin (1997:266), "limited agency" can explain the basic features of all the phenomena. This follows Braude (2003) who says the following:

"evidence provides a reasonable basis for believing in personal postmortem survival....it....clearly supports the belief that some do (survive death)" (2003:306).

At Gettysburg, that evidence must be the experience of documenting I.M.P. behaviors of the "culture of war" of the American Civil War in specific military spaces (K.O.C.O.A.). This is the "normative ghost culture" of the "Gettysburg (Civil War) Experience".

This I.M.P. behavior that led to a "normative ghost culture" was embedded in battle because of the unique composition of Civil War regiments: community-based companies consisting of friends, neighbors, relatives, brothers, and sometimes even fathers and sons. At Gettysburg, this unique composition was well represented. Here are two examples:

- Company F, 26th North Carolina: 50 men shared a surname with someone else in the regiment.
- Company G, 147th Pa.: There were nine sets of brothers, four first cousins, one father and son, and one uncle with two nephews.

Many died with these same individuals as companions in death. Thus, many soldiers died with a loved one at their side.

Many a family member initiated an arduous and expensive journey to the battlefield in the hope of obtaining closure offered by a proper burial at home (to achieve the "good death"). Many of these journeys, however, ended sadly. The mass of "unknowns" still buried on the battlefield attests to that journey of defeat. A consequence of this 19th c. belief system (the "good death"), and a death on the battlefield, without achieving it, led, I propose, to many manifestations that still haunt the Gettysburg battlefield today. It is these hauntings that become the Civil War "Gettysburg Experience".

Photo 23: The Rose Farm, the site of mass burials.

Photo 24: Another View of the Rose Farm

The "Hunt" for and the "Excavation" of Experience:

Thoughts on the 150ᵗʰ Anniversary of the Battle

Do We Re-Bury the "Dead" Again?

The "fog of war" was the primary sensory manifestation on the Gettysburg battlefield in 1863. The men (and women and boys) who fought that battle, both Northern and Southern, only saw for the most part tremendous amounts of smoke that effectively obscured the battlefield. Unfortunately, they heard more than they saw. What they heard was the constant, seemingly endless, yells and cries from the wounded and dying. This created only a narrow view of the battlefield, a view directly in front of them. This was their field of vision, and their sensory involvement in combat was largely an aural one. It was a "worm's eye" view of battle (Keegan 1976).

Today, most ghost "hunts" have yet to record this sonic element of battle: the shouts of anger, the curses of frustration, the cries of pain, the pleas for a mother's comfort, and the last gasps of dying men. Why is this? Do these sounds exist on today's Gettysburg battlefield? They do exist on Civil War battlefields. We have recorded them at Burnside Bridge at Antietam.

On a Civil War battlefield, soldiers knew little about the battle enveloping them, except for a narrow field of vision. Does this "worm's eye" view of the battle continue today among the ghost "hunts" at Gettysburg, and during those ghost tours in the town? Is a "fog of subjectivity" or a fog that clouds reasoning, obstructing the ghost hunting view of the Gettysburg Civil War experience?

This "fog" needs to be lifted before the Civil War experience can be felt and experienced at Gettysburg. The worms that once covered the dead in 1863, and ate away their vision of life, now "blind" the living in 2013. This blindness comes from a lack of understanding the ethnographic "culture of war" of these Civil War soldiers. It is the economics of power and entertainment that "fogs" our judgment of what is experienced on this battlefield.

As individuals investigating Civil War battlefields, we must remember that what these men fought for, what they believed, how they felt they should die, are not "dead" issues, lost in time. If Civil War soldiers are still "fighting" and "suffering" on the battlefield, then the experience of this "culture of war" is a history lesson, and a moral issue. It is not entertainment. It is certainly not a "ticket" to a TV show!

The "dead" at Gettysburg will long be remembered for what they are: DEAD – and not for what many believe they have become – GHOSTS! Their final performances ended long ago on a battlefield dedicated to their struggles. It is a battlefield seeped in the blood of their "last full measure". Let's remember that the next we have a "Gettysburg (Civil War) Experience"!

Gettysburg Requiem:
A Ritual Sonic Salute!

Just below the embedded defensive positions of the 20th Maine on Little Round Top, in a wooded area covered by rocky outcrops, there is the Company B marker of the 20th Maine (and the 2nd Pa. sharpshooters). There is a stone wall behind the marker. This was a cover and concealed position that was there during the battle in these woods on July 2, 1863. Behind this stone wall is the location where Captain Morrill of the 20th Maine, and members of the 2nd Pennsylvania sharpshooters, engaged the retreating soldiers of the 15th Alabama.

Many times have I come here, sometimes alone, and other times with a team of investigators. There are times we perform contextual acts during the day. At other times, we enact various scenarios at night.

Photo 25: The Location of the Company B Marker (Daylight)

Photo 26: The Location of the Company B Marker (Night)

There is a more fitting tribute to these men, both North and South, who fought and died in these woods than a small stone marker. It is something that we do after every investigation in these woods. I believe there is no more fitting tribute (or ritualistic act) than to send these "remaining" men "home" than an auditory performance, a musical set for a solemn ritual for the dead. Though it does not replace the ritual of the "good death", it is a therapeutic act to do, I believe, for both of us (those living and those still "living" the Civil War).

This type of performance is also entirely appropriate for an American Civil War battlefield, such as Gettysburg, because music and song were important elements of the "culture of war" (and probably all "cultures of war"). Music, song, and sounds were more important to 19th c. culture than they are today. According to Smith (2001):

"Aurality was important enough to contribute meaningfully and significantly to the construction of what it meant to be northern, southern, slave, or free in nineteenth-century America" (2001:6).

My own personal choice is to play Mary Fahl's "Going Home", a resonance to some aspects of the "good death", and the consequences of war that affected it's completion during the Civil War. Especially symbolic are the following lyrics:

"I know in my bones

I've been here before

The ground feels the same

Though the land's been torn.

I've a long way to go

The stars tell me so

On this road that will take me home.......

And when I pass by

Don't lead me astray

Don't try to stop me

Don't stand in my way

I'm bound for the hills

Where cool waters flow

On this road that will take me home".

There is no clearer description of a Civil War soldier than this: his longing to return "home". It also depicts the influence of the "good death", the longing for family in times of suffering and death. Finally, the lyrics, "don't stand in my way" reflect, for me, that resonance with the "culture of war" and its importance in the life of the Civil War soldier. "Don't stand in my way" means not to impose on these beliefs (such as with contemporary practices of ghost tours and "hunts", and a haunting experience as merely "entertainment" or something "entertaining"). To understand a Civil War haunting experience is to understand these words, and to use that understanding translated into respectable and sound fieldwork practices.

The song "Going Home" resonates, as music did, with the Civil War soldier. It is, in its least performative aspect, a message to those "ghost soldiers": it is now time to "go home". We play this song at the end of our investigation in the hopes of helping those who communicated with us, and who still remain, that it is now time to finally "cross-over". This use of music echoes the sentiments of others:

"If we listen to 'Juanita' or 'Home Again' from the band book of the 26th North Carolina, would we hear not only that desideratum we call history, but also perhaps – and they are one- ourselves as well? I think the spirits that observe us walk in music...." (Gramm 1994:179).

"I don't believe we can have an army without music

- **General Robert L. Lee**

Appendix:
A Haunted Gathering

Haunting experiences occur to ordinary people, not field technicians in white coats in a sterile laboratory. They occur as people are immersed in everyday social and interpersonal activities, ones that resonate with what occurred in a particular space, at a particular time in the past. This changes the concept of manifestation as an anomalous (and "paranormal") experience to one that is a human socio-cultural act and communicative event. As Robin Wooffitt (2010) has stated:

"….anomalous experiences, whatever their nature, are inextricably implicated in precisely the social processes and contexts which cannot be reproduced in laboratory conditions" (2010:73).

Is there a relationship between geographical variables and psi experiences (as "apparitional experience"), ones that are not related to geo-physical elements (electromagnetic or geomagnetic fields), or psychological factors (confirmation bias, belief)? Is there a relationship between these "apparitional experiences" and past geo-ethnographic data, such as "social" and "mental fields" (Sheldrake 2012) and the concept of "battle trance" (Jordania 2011)?

Are militarily-defined spaces on a battlefield (such as the K.O.C.O.A. configuration (see Sabol 2008) important to having an "apparitional experience"? Are certain cultures prone to haunting fields, such as the "culture of war" of the American Civil War? Do the distributions of psi phenomenon occur more frequently among certain designated populations of a particular culture in specific geographical spaces, such as Civil War regiments (the original "band of brothers") of the "culture of war" in specific K.O.C.O.A. spaces?

The "spirit hypothesis" proposes that **"an apparition is a real, localized externalized entity, and not simply a subjective construct of the percipient" (Braude 1991:194).**

Some apparitions are seen (and experienced) repeatedly and independently by different people over time in the same location. Does this occur on the Gettysburg battlefield in a consistent <u>and</u> contextually <u>sound</u> manner? The final question of an "afterlife consciousness", focused on a "Gettysburg (Civil War) Experience" is whether the manifestations of reported apparitions conform to the "culture of war", its I.M.P. behaviors, of the American Civil War; and whether these manifestations are contextual to known behaviors that would have been enacted in particular battlefield K.O.C.O.A. spaces.

If the answer is affirmative, occurs on a consistent basis from reliable eye and earwitnesses, and is recorded, then we <u>can</u> document these experiences as those coming from Civil War soldiers who fought (and died) at Gettysburg in July of 1863. The "truth" is out there on the battlefield!

Bibliography

Auge, Marc (1998). *A Sense for the Other: The Timelessness and Relevance of Anthropology.* Stanford: Stanford University Press.

Asfar, Dan and Edrick Thay (2004). *Ghost Stories of the Civil War.* Edmonton: Ghost House Books.

Belanger, Jeff (2005). *Ghosts of War.* Franklin Lakes, New Jersey: Career Press.

Boal, Augusto (1985). *Theatre of the Oppressed.* New York: Theatre Communication Group.

Braude, Stephen E. (1991). "Apparitions" in S. E. Braude, *The Limits of Influence: Psychokinesis and The Philosophy of Science.* London: Routledge. pp. 170-218.

(2003). *Immortal Remains: The Evidence for Life After Death.* U.K. : Littlefield Publishing, Inc.

Cardena, E. and D. Spiegel (1991). "Suggestibility, Absorption, and Disassociation: An Integrative Model of Hypnosis" in J.F. Schumaker (Editor) *Human Suggestion: Advances in Theory, Research, and Application.* New York: Routledge. pp. 93-107.

Coco, Gregory A. (1995). *A Strange and Blighted Land.* Gettysburg: Thomas Publications.

DeNardi, Sarah (2007). "Whose Genius Loci? Worling Across Disciplines in the Exploration of 'Spirit of Place' on Monte Altare, Northeast Italy". Paper Presented at the Theoretical Archaeology Group (T.A.G.) Conference, York, England.

Eiseley, Loren (1971). *The Night Country.* New York: Charles Scribner's Sons.

Faust, Drew Gilpin (2008). *This Republic of Suffering: Death and the American Civil War.* New York: Alfred A. Knopf.

Frassanito, William (1975). *Gettysburg: A Journey in Time.* Gettysburg: Thomas Publications.

Fussel, Paul (2008). "Reflections on the Culture of War" in *Battle: The Nature and Consequences of Civil War Combat.* Kent Gramm (Editor). Tuscaloosa: University of Alabama Press. pp. 12-66.

Glassie, Henry (1977). "Archaeology and Folklore: Common Anxieties, Common Hopes" in *Historical Archaeology and the Importance of Material Things. Leland Ferguson (Editor). Special Publication Series No. 2: 23-35. California, Pennsylvania: Society for Historical Archaeology.*

Gramm, Kent (1994). *Gettysburg: A Meditation on War and Values.* Bloomington: University of Indiana Press.

Griffin, D. R. (1997). *Parapsychology, Philosophy, and Spirituality: A Postmodern Exploration.* Albany: State University of New York Press.

Haskell, Frank (1908). *The Battle of Gettysburg.* Madison: Wisconsin Historical Commission.

Jordania, Joseph (2011). *Why Do People Sing? Music in Human Evolution.* Logos.

Keegan, John (1976). *The Face of Battle.*

Lange, R. and J. Houran (1997). "Context-Induced Paranormal Experience: Support for Houran and Lange's Model of Haunting Phenomenon". *Perceptual and Motor Skills* 84: 1455-58.

Law, John and AnneMarie Mol (2002). *Complexities: Social Studies of Knowledge Practices*. Durham, North Carolina: Duke University Press.

Laxness, Halldor (1997). *Independent People*. Vintage Books.

Lesser, Alexander (1961). "Social Fields and the Evolution of Society". *Southwestern Journal of Anthropology*. 17: 40-48.

Leone, Mark and Parker B. Potter (1988). "The Recovery of Meaning: Historical Archaeology in the Eastern United States". Washington, D.C. : Smithsonian Institution Press.

Lowenthal, David (1985). *The Past is a Foreign Country*. Cambridge: Cambridge University Press.

McClenon, J. "The Sociological Investigation of Haunting Cases" in J. Houran and R. Lange (Editors) *Hauntings and Poltergeists: Multi-Disciplinary Perspectives*. Jefferson, North Carolina: McFarland. pp. 62-81.

McRandle, James (1944). *The Antique Drums of War*. College Station: Texas A&M Press.

Mitchell, Reid (1995). *The Vacant Chair: The Northern Soldier Leaves Home*. Oxford University Press.

Nesbitt, Mark and Katherine Ramsland (2012). *Paranormal Forensics Investigators*. Gettysburg: Second Chance Publications.

Quinton, A. (1975). "The Soul" in J. Perry (Editor) *Personal Identity*. Berkeley: University of California Press. pp. 52-72.

Roach, J. (1996). *Cities of the Dead: Circum-Atlantic Performances*. New York: Columbia University Press.

Runia, Eelco (2006). "Spots of Time" *History and Theory*. 45(3): 305-316.

Sabol, John G. (2007). *Ghost Excavator: Unearthing the Drama in the Mine Fields*. Bloomington, Indiana: AuthorHouse.

(2007). *Ghost Culture*. Bloomington, Indiana: AuthorHouse.

(2007). *Gettysburg Unearthed*. *Bloomington, Indiana: AuthorHouse*.

(2008). Battlefield Hauntscape. Bloomington, Indiana: AuthorHouse.

(2008). *The Politics of Presence*. Bloomington, Indiana: AuthorHouse.

(2009). *Phantom Gettysburg*. Bloomington, Indiana: AuthorHouse.

(2010). *The Re-Haunting(s) of Gettysburg*. Bloomington, Indiana: AuthorHouse.

(2012). *Ghost Culture Too*. Bloomington, Indiana: AuthorHouse.

Shanks, Michael (2012). *The Archaeological Imagination*. Walnut Creek, California: Left Coast Press.

Sheldrake, Rupert (2012). *The Science Delusion: Freeing the Spirit of Enquiry*. London: Hodder & Stoughton, Ltd.

Smith, Mark N. (2001). *Listening to Nineteenth Century America*. Chapel Hill: University of North Carolina Press.

Tilly, Christopher (1999). *Metaphor and Material Culture*. Oxford: Blackwell.

Willey, Gordon R. and Philip Phillips (1958). *Method and Theory in American Archaeology*. Chicago: University of Chicago Press.

Williams, Raymond (1977). *Marxism and Literature*. Oxford: Oxford University Press.

Wolf, Eric (1984). "Culture: Panacea or Problem". *American Antiquity*. 49: 393-400.

Wooffitt, Robin (2010). "Toward a Sociological Parapsychology" in *Anomalous Experiences: Essays from Parapsychology and Psychological Perspectives*. Matthew D. Smith (Editor). Jefferson, North Carolina: McFarland. pp. 72-91.

Biography

John Sabol is an archaeologist, cultural anthropologist, actor, and author. As an archaeologist, he has unearthed past material remains in excavations and site surveys in England, Mexico, and at various sites in the United States (including Eastern South Dakota, the Tennessee River Valleys, and in Pennsylvania). His anthropological fieldwork includes the studies of "spirits" in the religious beliefs of the afterlife among various cultural groups in Mexico (Mixtec, Zapotec, Lacandon, Nahuatl, and Otomi). His acting career includes "ghosting" performances of various characters and scenarios in more than 35 movies, TV shows, and documentaries. He has appeared in the A&E TV series, Paranormal State as an investigative consultant.

He has written sixteen books. These include: *Ghost Excavator (2007), Ghost Culture (2007), Gettysburg Unearthed (2007), Battlefield Hauntscape (2008), The Anthracite Coal Region: The Archaeology of its Haunting Presence (2008), The Politics of Presence: Haunting Performances on the Gettysburg Battlefield (2008), Bodies of Substance, Fragments of Memories: An Archaeological Sensitivity to Ghostly Presence (2009), Phantom Gettysburg (2009), Digging Deep: An Archaeologist Unearths a Haunted Life (2009), The Re-Hauntings of Gettysburg (2010), Digging Up Ghosts (2011), The Haunted Theatre (2011), Haunting Archaeologies (2012), Beyond the Paranormal: Unearthing An Extended "Normal" at Haunted Locations (2013), Burnside Bridge Hauntscape: The Excavation of a Civil War Soundscape (2013), and The Gettysburg Battlefield Experience (2013).*

His recent speaking engagements include the T.A.G. (Theoretical Archaeology Group) Conference at the University of California, Berkeley, at the Space and Place Conference in Prague, Czech Republic, the TAG Conference at the University in Buffalo, New York, Exploring the Extraordinary Conference in York, England, the

C.H.A.T. archaeological conference also in York, and the GHost Conference at the University of London, London, England.

His investigative reports have been published in such diverse venues as Haunted Times Magazine, Tennessee Anthropologist, and the online journal, ParaAnthropology. He has been a frequent guest on numerous radio and internet talk shows, among them, Beyond the Edge Radio, The Paranormal View, Para X Radio, Blog Talk Radio, The Grand Dark Conspiracy, and Rusty O'Nhiall's "Mysterious and Unexplained" on PsiFM (Australia). He was a university professor in Mexico for 11 years, teaching both undergraduate and graduate courses on the anthropology of tourism. He has also been featured on public educational TV for U.S. and foreign markets, and has worked on international educational documentaries (in Spain).

He has a M.A. in Anthropology/Archaeology (University of Tennessee), and a B.A. in Sociology/Anthropology (Bloomsburg University). He has also attended Penn State University, the University of Pittsburgh, the University of the Americas (Cholula, Puebla, Mexico), and has studied theatre and method acting in Mexico City.

He can be reached via email at cuicospirit@hotmail.com. His website is: **www.ghostexcavation.com** and he can be found on Facebook ("Ghost Excavations with John Sabol").

27. The Author at Gettysburg.